# 50 Healthy and Hearty Recipes for Home

By: Kelly Johnson

# Table of Contents

- Quinoa and Black Bean Stuffed Peppers
- Sweet Potato and Chickpea Curry
- Grilled Salmon with Avocado Salsa
- Lentil and Spinach Stew
- Chicken and Vegetable Stir-Fry
- Mediterranean Quinoa Salad
- Baked Cod with Lemon and Dill
- Butternut Squash and Kale Risotto
- Spicy Turkey and Bean Chili
- Roasted Veggie Power Bowl
- Tofu and Broccoli Teriyaki
- Moroccan Chicken Tagine
- Veggie-Packed Minestrone Soup
- Spinach and Feta Stuffed Chicken Breast
- Thai Peanut Quinoa Bowl
- Beef and Sweet Potato Stew
- Mediterranean Baked Cod
- Zucchini Noodles with Pesto and Cherry Tomatoes
- Cauliflower Rice Stir-Fry
- Turkey and Quinoa Stuffed Bell Peppers
- Shrimp and Avocado Salad
- Hearty Lentil Soup
- Baked Lemon Herb Chicken
- Quinoa and Veggie Stuffed Acorn Squash
- Spaghetti Squash with Marinara Sauce
- Seared Tuna with Mango Salsa
- Black Bean and Corn Salad
- Chicken and Wild Rice Soup
- Grilled Veggie and Quinoa Bowl
- Mushroom and Barley Soup
- Chickpea and Spinach Stew
- Almond-Crusted Baked Chicken
- Sweet Potato and Black Bean Tacos
- Garlic Shrimp and Broccoli
- Vegan Buddha Bowl

- Greek Chicken and Vegetable Skewers
- Stuffed Portobello Mushrooms
- Cabbage and Beef Soup
- Roasted Cauliflower and Chickpea Tacos
- Chicken and Avocado Salad
- Spinach and Quinoa Stuffed Bell Peppers
- Baked Salmon with Asparagus
- Vegetable and Lentil Shepherd's Pie
- Chicken and Mushroom Stroganoff
- Eggplant and Chickpea Stew
- Tuna and White Bean Salad
- Lemon Garlic Chicken and Green Beans
- Veggie-Packed Quinoa Pilaf
- Balsamic Glazed Roasted Vegetables
- Spiced Lentil and Carrot Soup

**Quinoa and Black Bean Stuffed Peppers**

Ingredients:

- 4 large bell peppers (any color)
- 1 cup quinoa, rinsed
- 1 3/4 cups vegetable broth or water
- 1 can (15 oz) black beans, drained and rinsed
- 1 cup corn kernels (fresh or frozen)
- 1 small red onion, finely chopped
- 2 cloves garlic, minced
- 1 can (14.5 oz) diced tomatoes, drained
- 1 teaspoon ground cumin
- 1 teaspoon chili powder
- 1/2 teaspoon paprika
- Salt and pepper to taste
- 1 cup shredded cheese (cheddar, mozzarella, or your choice) – optional
- Fresh cilantro, chopped (for garnish)
- Lime wedges (for serving)

Instructions:

Preheat Oven:

1. Preheat your oven to 375°F (190°C).

Prepare the Bell Peppers:

2. Cut the tops off the bell peppers and remove the seeds and membranes. If needed, trim the bottoms slightly to help them stand upright. Place them in a baking dish.

Cook the Quinoa:

3. In a medium saucepan, bring the quinoa and vegetable broth or water to a boil. Reduce heat, cover, and simmer for about 15 minutes, or until the quinoa is cooked and the liquid is absorbed. Fluff with a fork.

Prepare the Filling:

4. In a large mixing bowl, combine the cooked quinoa, black beans, corn, red onion, garlic, diced tomatoes, cumin, chili powder, paprika, salt, and pepper. Mix well.

Stuff the Peppers:

5. Spoon the quinoa mixture into the bell peppers, packing it in tightly. If using, sprinkle shredded cheese on top of each stuffed pepper.

Bake:

6. Cover the baking dish with foil and bake for 30 minutes. Remove the foil and bake for an additional 10-15 minutes, until the peppers are tender and the cheese is melted and bubbly.

Serve:

7. Garnish with fresh cilantro and serve with lime wedges.

Enjoy your healthy and hearty Quinoa and Black Bean Stuffed Peppers!

**Sweet Potato and Chickpea Curry**

Ingredients:

- 2 large sweet potatoes, peeled and diced
- 1 can (15 oz) chickpeas, drained and rinsed
- 1 large onion, finely chopped
- 3 cloves garlic, minced
- 1 tablespoon fresh ginger, grated
- 1 can (14.5 oz) diced tomatoes
- 1 can (14 oz) coconut milk
- 2 tablespoons curry powder
- 1 teaspoon ground cumin
- 1 teaspoon ground coriander
- 1/2 teaspoon ground turmeric
- 1/4 teaspoon cayenne pepper (optional)
- Salt and pepper to taste
- 2 tablespoons olive oil or coconut oil
- Fresh cilantro, chopped (for garnish)
- Cooked rice or naan (for serving)

Instructions:

Prepare the Ingredients:

1. Peel and dice the sweet potatoes into bite-sized pieces. Finely chop the onion, mince the garlic, and grate the fresh ginger.

Cook the Aromatics:

2. In a large pot or Dutch oven, heat the olive oil over medium heat. Add the chopped onion and cook until it becomes translucent, about 5-7 minutes. Add the minced garlic and grated ginger, and cook for another 2 minutes until fragrant.

Add the Spices:

3. Stir in the curry powder, ground cumin, ground coriander, ground turmeric, and cayenne pepper (if using). Cook the spices with the onion mixture for 1-2 minutes to release their flavors.

Add Sweet Potatoes and Chickpeas:

4. Add the diced sweet potatoes and drained chickpeas to the pot, stirring to coat them with the spice mixture.

Add Tomatoes and Coconut Milk:

5. Pour in the diced tomatoes (with their juices) and the coconut milk. Stir well to combine all the ingredients.

Simmer the Curry:

6. Bring the mixture to a boil, then reduce the heat to low and let it simmer, covered, for about 20-25 minutes, or until the sweet potatoes are tender and the flavors have melded together. Stir occasionally to prevent sticking.

Season and Serve:

7. Season the curry with salt and pepper to taste. Garnish with chopped fresh cilantro.

Serve:

8. Serve the sweet potato and chickpea curry over cooked rice or with naan bread.

Enjoy your hearty and flavorful Sweet Potato and Chickpea Curry!

**Grilled Salmon with Avocado Salsa**

Ingredients:

For the Salmon:

- 4 salmon fillets (about 6 oz each)
- 2 tablespoons olive oil
- 2 cloves garlic, minced
- 1 teaspoon ground cumin
- 1 teaspoon smoked paprika
- Salt and pepper to taste
- 1 lime, juiced

For the Avocado Salsa:

- 2 ripe avocados, diced
- 1 small red onion, finely chopped
- 1 jalapeño, seeded and finely chopped (optional)
- 1 cup cherry tomatoes, quartered
- 1/4 cup fresh cilantro, chopped
- 1 lime, juiced
- Salt and pepper to taste

Instructions:

Prepare the Marinade:

1. In a small bowl, combine the olive oil, minced garlic, ground cumin, smoked paprika, salt, pepper, and lime juice. Mix well to create the marinade.

Marinate the Salmon:

2. Place the salmon fillets in a shallow dish and pour the marinade over them, ensuring each fillet is well-coated. Let the salmon marinate for at least 15-20 minutes.

Preheat the Grill:

3. Preheat your grill to medium-high heat. Make sure the grates are clean and lightly oiled to prevent sticking.

Grill the Salmon:

4. Place the salmon fillets on the grill, skin side down if they have skin. Grill for about 4-5 minutes per side, or until the salmon is opaque and flakes easily with a fork. Cooking time may vary depending on the thickness of the fillets.

Prepare the Avocado Salsa:

5. While the salmon is grilling, prepare the avocado salsa. In a medium bowl, gently combine the diced avocados, chopped red onion, jalapeño (if using), cherry tomatoes, fresh cilantro, lime juice, salt, and pepper. Mix well but carefully to keep the avocado pieces intact.

Serve:

6. Once the salmon is done, transfer the fillets to serving plates. Top each fillet with a generous spoonful of avocado salsa.

Enjoy your healthy and delicious Grilled Salmon with Avocado Salsa!

**Lentil and Spinach Stew**

Ingredients:

- 1 cup green or brown lentils, rinsed and drained
- 1 tablespoon olive oil
- 1 large onion, finely chopped
- 2 cloves garlic, minced
- 2 carrots, diced
- 2 celery stalks, diced
- 1 large potato, peeled and diced
- 1 can (14.5 oz) diced tomatoes
- 4 cups vegetable broth
- 1 teaspoon ground cumin
- 1 teaspoon ground coriander
- 1/2 teaspoon smoked paprika
- 1/4 teaspoon cayenne pepper (optional)
- Salt and pepper to taste
- 4 cups fresh spinach, roughly chopped
- 2 tablespoons lemon juice
- Fresh parsley, chopped (for garnish)

Instructions:

Prepare the Vegetables:

1. Finely chop the onion, mince the garlic, and dice the carrots, celery, and potato.

Cook the Aromatics:

2. In a large pot or Dutch oven, heat the olive oil over medium heat. Add the chopped onion and cook until it becomes translucent, about 5-7 minutes. Add the minced garlic and cook for another 1-2 minutes until fragrant.

Add the Vegetables:

3. Stir in the diced carrots, celery, and potato. Cook for about 5 minutes, stirring occasionally.

**Add Spices and Tomatoes:**

4. Add the ground cumin, ground coriander, smoked paprika, and cayenne pepper (if using). Stir well to coat the vegetables with the spices. Add the diced tomatoes and cook for another 2-3 minutes.

**Add Lentils and Broth:**

5. Add the lentils to the pot, then pour in the vegetable broth. Stir to combine all the ingredients.

**Simmer the Stew:**

6. Bring the mixture to a boil, then reduce the heat to low and let it simmer, covered, for about 30-35 minutes, or until the lentils and vegetables are tender. Stir occasionally to prevent sticking.

**Add Spinach:**

7. Stir in the chopped fresh spinach and cook for an additional 5 minutes, or until the spinach is wilted and well incorporated into the stew.

**Finish with Lemon Juice:**

8. Add the lemon juice and season the stew with salt and pepper to taste. Stir well to combine.

**Serve:**

9. Ladle the stew into bowls and garnish with fresh parsley.

Enjoy your hearty and healthy Lentil and Spinach Stew!

**Chicken and Vegetable Stir-Fry**

Ingredients:

For the Stir-Fry:

- 1 lb chicken breast, thinly sliced
- 2 tablespoons soy sauce (or tamari for gluten-free)
- 1 tablespoon cornstarch
- 1 tablespoon olive oil or sesame oil
- 1 red bell pepper, thinly sliced
- 1 yellow bell pepper, thinly sliced
- 1 large carrot, julienned
- 1 cup broccoli florets
- 1 cup snap peas
- 1 small red onion, thinly sliced
- 3 cloves garlic, minced
- 1 tablespoon fresh ginger, grated

For the Sauce:

- 1/4 cup soy sauce (or tamari for gluten-free)
- 2 tablespoons hoisin sauce
- 2 tablespoons rice vinegar
- 1 tablespoon honey or maple syrup
- 1 tablespoon cornstarch mixed with 2 tablespoons water (optional, for thickening)
- 1/4 cup water

Garnish:

- Sesame seeds
- Green onions, sliced

Instructions:

**Marinate the Chicken:**

1. In a bowl, combine the sliced chicken with 2 tablespoons of soy sauce and 1 tablespoon of cornstarch. Mix well and let it marinate for at least 15 minutes.

**Prepare the Sauce:**

2. In a small bowl, whisk together the 1/4 cup soy sauce, hoisin sauce, rice vinegar, honey (or maple syrup), and water. If you prefer a thicker sauce, add the cornstarch slurry (1 tablespoon cornstarch mixed with 2 tablespoons water) to the sauce mixture.

**Cook the Chicken:**

3. Heat 1 tablespoon of olive oil (or sesame oil) in a large skillet or wok over medium-high heat. Add the marinated chicken and cook until it's no longer pink and slightly browned, about 5-7 minutes. Remove the chicken from the skillet and set it aside.

**Stir-Fry the Vegetables:**

4. In the same skillet, add a bit more oil if needed. Add the garlic and ginger, and stir-fry for about 30 seconds until fragrant. Add the red bell pepper, yellow bell pepper, carrot, broccoli, snap peas, and red onion. Stir-fry for 5-7 minutes, or until the vegetables are tender-crisp.

**Combine Chicken and Sauce:**

5. Return the cooked chicken to the skillet with the vegetables. Pour the sauce over the mixture and stir well to combine. Cook for an additional 2-3 minutes, allowing the sauce to thicken and coat the chicken and vegetables evenly.

**Serve:**

6. Remove from heat and garnish with sesame seeds and sliced green onions. Serve the chicken and vegetable stir-fry over cooked rice or noodles.

Enjoy your healthy and delicious Chicken and Vegetable Stir-Fry!

**Mediterranean Quinoa Salad**

Ingredients:

- 1 cup quinoa, rinsed and drained
- 2 cups water or vegetable broth
- 1 can (15 oz) chickpeas, drained and rinsed
- 1 cup cherry tomatoes, halved
- 1 cucumber, diced
- 1 red bell pepper, diced
- 1/4 red onion, finely chopped
- 1/2 cup Kalamata olives, pitted and halved
- 1/2 cup crumbled feta cheese (optional)
- 1/4 cup fresh parsley, chopped
- 1/4 cup fresh mint, chopped

For the Dressing:

- 1/4 cup extra-virgin olive oil
- 2 tablespoons red wine vinegar
- 1 tablespoon lemon juice
- 1 clove garlic, minced
- 1 teaspoon dried oregano
- Salt and pepper to taste

Instructions:

Cook the Quinoa:

1. In a medium saucepan, combine the quinoa and water (or vegetable broth). Bring to a boil, then reduce the heat to low, cover, and simmer for about 15 minutes, or until the quinoa is cooked and the liquid is absorbed. Remove from heat and let it sit, covered, for 5 minutes. Fluff with a fork and let it cool.

Prepare the Vegetables:

2. While the quinoa is cooling, prepare the vegetables. Halve the cherry tomatoes, dice the cucumber and red bell pepper, finely chop the red onion, and halve the Kalamata olives.

Make the Dressing:

3. In a small bowl, whisk together the olive oil, red wine vinegar, lemon juice, minced garlic, dried oregano, salt, and pepper until well combined.

Assemble the Salad:

4. In a large bowl, combine the cooked quinoa, chickpeas, cherry tomatoes, cucumber, red bell pepper, red onion, and Kalamata olives. Pour the dressing over the salad and toss to combine.

Add Herbs and Cheese:

5. Gently fold in the chopped parsley, mint, and crumbled feta cheese (if using).

Serve:

6. Serve immediately, or chill in the refrigerator for 30 minutes to allow the flavors to meld together. This salad can be served on its own or as a side dish.

Enjoy your fresh and flavorful Mediterranean Quinoa Salad!

**Baked Cod with Lemon and Dill**

Ingredients:

- 4 cod fillets (about 6 oz each)
- 2 tablespoons olive oil
- 1 lemon, thinly sliced
- 2 tablespoons fresh lemon juice
- 3 cloves garlic, minced
- 1 tablespoon fresh dill, chopped (or 1 teaspoon dried dill)
- Salt and pepper to taste
- 1/2 teaspoon paprika
- Fresh dill sprigs (for garnish)
- Lemon wedges (for serving)

Instructions:

Preheat Oven:

1. Preheat your oven to 400°F (200°C). Line a baking dish with parchment paper or lightly grease it with olive oil.

Prepare the Cod Fillets:

2. Pat the cod fillets dry with paper towels and place them in the prepared baking dish. Drizzle the fillets with olive oil and fresh lemon juice.

Season the Cod:

3. Sprinkle the minced garlic, chopped dill, salt, pepper, and paprika evenly over the fillets. Arrange the lemon slices on top of and around the cod fillets.

Bake:

4. Bake in the preheated oven for 12-15 minutes, or until the cod is opaque and flakes easily with a fork. The exact cooking time will depend on the thickness of the fillets.

Serve:

5. Garnish the baked cod with fresh dill sprigs and serve with lemon wedges on the side.

Enjoy your healthy and flavorful Baked Cod with Lemon and Dill!

**Butternut Squash and Kale Risotto**

Ingredients:

- 1 small butternut squash, peeled, seeded, and diced into small cubes
- 1 bunch kale, stems removed and leaves chopped
- 1 1/2 cups Arborio rice
- 4 cups vegetable broth
- 1 onion, finely chopped
- 2 cloves garlic, minced
- 1/2 cup dry white wine (optional)
- 1/2 cup grated Parmesan cheese (optional)
- 2 tablespoons olive oil
- Salt and pepper to taste
- Fresh parsley, chopped (for garnish)

Instructions:

Prepare the Ingredients:

1. Peel, seed, and dice the butternut squash into small cubes. Remove the stems from the kale and chop the leaves. Finely chop the onion and mince the garlic.

Cook the Butternut Squash:

2. Heat 1 tablespoon of olive oil in a large skillet or pan over medium heat. Add the diced butternut squash and cook, stirring occasionally, until it's tender and lightly browned, about 10-12 minutes. Remove the squash from the pan and set it aside.

Prepare the Risotto Base:

3. In the same pan, heat another tablespoon of olive oil over medium heat. Add the chopped onion and cook until it becomes translucent, about 5-7 minutes. Add the minced garlic and cook for another minute until fragrant.

Toast the Rice:

4. Add the Arborio rice to the pan with the onion and garlic. Stir the rice constantly for about 2-3 minutes until it's lightly toasted.

Add the Wine (Optional):

5. If using white wine, pour it into the pan with the rice and stir until it's absorbed.

Cook the Risotto:

6. Begin adding the vegetable broth to the rice mixture, one ladleful at a time, stirring frequently. Allow each ladleful of broth to be absorbed before adding the next. Continue this process until the rice is creamy and tender, which should take about 20-25 minutes.

Add the Butternut Squash and Kale:

7. During the last 5 minutes of cooking, add the cooked butternut squash and chopped kale to the risotto. Stir well to combine and allow the kale to wilt.

Finish the Risotto:

8. Once the risotto is cooked and creamy, remove it from the heat. Stir in the grated Parmesan cheese (if using) and season with salt and pepper to taste.

Serve:

9. Garnish the butternut squash and kale risotto with chopped fresh parsley. Serve hot and enjoy!

This Butternut Squash and Kale Risotto makes for a comforting and nutritious meal that's perfect for cooler days.

**Spicy Turkey and Bean Chili**

Ingredients:

- 1 lb ground turkey
- 1 onion, chopped
- 3 cloves garlic, minced
- 1 bell pepper, diced
- 1 jalapeño pepper, seeded and minced (adjust to taste)
- 2 cans (14.5 oz each) diced tomatoes
- 2 cans (15 oz each) kidney beans, drained and rinsed
- 1 can (15 oz) black beans, drained and rinsed
- 1 can (6 oz) tomato paste
- 2 cups chicken or vegetable broth
- 2 tablespoons chili powder
- 1 tablespoon ground cumin
- 1 teaspoon smoked paprika
- 1 teaspoon dried oregano
- Salt and pepper to taste
- Olive oil for cooking
- Optional toppings: shredded cheese, sour cream, chopped cilantro, sliced green onions, avocado slices

Instructions:

Cook the Turkey:

1. Heat a large pot or Dutch oven over medium heat. Add a drizzle of olive oil and the ground turkey. Cook, breaking it up with a spoon, until browned and cooked through, about 5-7 minutes.

Saute Aromatics:

2. Add the chopped onion, minced garlic, diced bell pepper, and minced jalapeño pepper to the pot with the turkey. Cook, stirring occasionally, until the vegetables are softened, about 5 minutes.

Add Tomatoes and Beans:

3. Stir in the diced tomatoes, kidney beans, black beans, and tomato paste.

Season:

4. Add the chili powder, ground cumin, smoked paprika, dried oregano, salt, and pepper to the pot. Stir well to combine.

Simmer:

5. Pour in the chicken or vegetable broth and stir to combine. Bring the chili to a simmer.

Cook:

6. Reduce the heat to low and let the chili simmer, uncovered, for about 20-30 minutes, stirring occasionally, to allow the flavors to meld together and the chili to thicken to your desired consistency.

Adjust Seasoning:

7. Taste the chili and adjust the seasoning with more salt, pepper, or spices if needed.

Serve:

8. Ladle the spicy turkey and bean chili into bowls and serve hot. Optionally, top each serving with shredded cheese, a dollop of sour cream, chopped cilantro, sliced green onions, or avocado slices.

Enjoy your hearty and flavorful Spicy Turkey and Bean Chili!

**Roasted Veggie Power Bowl**

Ingredients:

For the Roasted Vegetables:

- 1 small sweet potato, peeled and diced
- 1 cup broccoli florets
- 1 cup cauliflower florets
- 1 red bell pepper, sliced
- 1 yellow bell pepper, sliced
- 1 small red onion, sliced
- 2 tablespoons olive oil
- 1 teaspoon garlic powder
- 1 teaspoon smoked paprika
- Salt and pepper to taste

For the Power Bowl:

- 1 cup cooked quinoa or brown rice
- 1 cup cooked chickpeas
- 2 cups fresh spinach or kale, chopped
- 1 avocado, sliced
- Lemon wedges (for serving)
- Tahini or your favorite dressing (optional)

Instructions:

Preheat Oven:

1. Preheat your oven to 425°F (220°C). Line a baking sheet with parchment paper or aluminum foil.

Prepare the Vegetables:

2. In a large mixing bowl, toss the diced sweet potato, broccoli florets, cauliflower florets, sliced red bell pepper, sliced yellow bell pepper, and sliced red onion with olive oil, garlic powder, smoked paprika, salt, and pepper until evenly coated.

Roast the Vegetables:

3. Spread the seasoned vegetables out in a single layer on the prepared baking sheet. Roast in the preheated oven for 20-25 minutes, or until the vegetables are tender and lightly browned, stirring halfway through the cooking time.

Assemble the Power Bowl:

4. In serving bowls, layer cooked quinoa or brown rice, roasted vegetables, cooked chickpeas, and chopped spinach or kale. Top with sliced avocado.

Serve:

5. Squeeze fresh lemon juice over the power bowls before serving. Optionally, drizzle with tahini or your favorite dressing for extra flavor.

Enjoy!

6. Enjoy your vibrant and nutritious Roasted Veggie Power Bowl as a satisfying and wholesome meal.

Feel free to customize your power bowl with your favorite vegetables, grains, proteins, and toppings for endless variations!

**Tofu and Broccoli Teriyaki**

Ingredients:

- 1 block (14 oz) firm tofu, pressed and cubed
- 2 cups broccoli florets
- 2 tablespoons sesame oil or vegetable oil
- 3 cloves garlic, minced
- 1 tablespoon fresh ginger, grated
- 1/4 cup soy sauce (or tamari for gluten-free option)
- 2 tablespoons rice vinegar
- 2 tablespoons honey or maple syrup
- 2 tablespoons water
- 1 tablespoon cornstarch
- Cooked rice, for serving
- Sesame seeds and sliced green onions, for garnish (optional)

Instructions:

Prepare the Tofu:

1. Press the tofu to remove excess water. Cut the pressed tofu into cubes and set aside.

Blanch the Broccoli:

2. Bring a pot of water to a boil and blanch the broccoli florets for 1-2 minutes. Drain and set aside.

Make the Teriyaki Sauce:

3. In a small bowl, whisk together soy sauce, rice vinegar, honey or maple syrup, water, and cornstarch until smooth. Set aside.

Cook the Tofu:

4. Heat 1 tablespoon of sesame oil (or vegetable oil) in a large skillet or wok over medium-high heat. Add the cubed tofu and cook until golden brown on all sides, about 5-7 minutes. Remove the tofu from the skillet and set aside.

**Stir-Fry Garlic and Ginger:**

5. In the same skillet, add the remaining tablespoon of sesame oil (or vegetable oil) if needed. Add minced garlic and grated ginger, and stir-fry for about 1 minute until fragrant.

**Combine Tofu and Broccoli:**

6. Return the cooked tofu to the skillet. Add blanched broccoli florets to the skillet with tofu.

**Add Teriyaki Sauce:**

7. Pour the teriyaki sauce over the tofu and broccoli. Stir well to coat everything evenly with the sauce.

**Simmer:**

8. Reduce the heat to medium-low and let the tofu and broccoli simmer in the teriyaki sauce for 2-3 minutes, or until the sauce has thickened slightly.

**Serve:**

9. Serve the tofu and broccoli teriyaki over cooked rice. Garnish with sesame seeds and sliced green onions if desired.

Enjoy your flavorful Tofu and Broccoli Teriyaki served over rice for a satisfying meal!

**Moroccan Chicken Tagine**

Ingredients:

- 4 chicken thighs, bone-in and skin-on
- 1 large onion, chopped
- 3 cloves garlic, minced
- 1 tablespoon fresh ginger, grated
- 2 carrots, peeled and sliced
- 1 preserved lemon, chopped (optional)
- 1 cup green olives, pitted
- 1 teaspoon ground cumin
- 1 teaspoon ground coriander
- 1 teaspoon ground cinnamon
- 1/2 teaspoon ground turmeric
- 1/2 teaspoon paprika
- 1/4 teaspoon cayenne pepper (optional, for extra heat)
- 1 can (14 oz) diced tomatoes
- 1 cup chicken broth
- 2 tablespoons olive oil
- Salt and pepper to taste
- Fresh cilantro, chopped (for garnish)
- Cooked couscous or crusty bread (for serving)

Instructions:

Brown the Chicken:

1. Season the chicken thighs with salt and pepper. Heat olive oil in a large tagine or Dutch oven over medium-high heat. Brown the chicken thighs on both sides until golden, about 5 minutes per side. Remove the chicken from the tagine and set aside.

Saute Aromatics:

2. In the same tagine or Dutch oven, add chopped onion and cook until softened, about 5 minutes. Add minced garlic and grated ginger, and cook for another 1-2 minutes until fragrant.

Add Spices:

3. Stir in ground cumin, ground coriander, ground cinnamon, ground turmeric, paprika, and cayenne pepper (if using). Cook the spices with the onion mixture for 1-2 minutes to release their flavors.

Simmer with Tomatoes:

4. Add diced tomatoes (with their juices) to the tagine, stirring well to combine. Allow the mixture to simmer for a few minutes.

Return Chicken to Tagine:

5. Return the browned chicken thighs to the tagine, nestling them into the sauce.

Add Carrots and Preserved Lemon:

6. Add sliced carrots and chopped preserved lemon (if using) to the tagine. Stir to distribute the ingredients evenly.

Add Chicken Broth and Olives:

7. Pour chicken broth over the chicken and vegetables. Add green olives to the tagine, distributing them throughout.

Simmer:

8. Cover the tagine with a lid and reduce the heat to low. Allow the chicken to simmer gently in the sauce for about 45-60 minutes, or until the chicken is tender and cooked through, and the flavors have melded together.

Serve:

9. Serve the Moroccan Chicken Tagine hot, garnished with chopped fresh cilantro. Serve with cooked couscous or crusty bread on the side.

Enjoy the rich and aromatic flavors of this Moroccan Chicken Tagine!

**Veggie-Packed Minestrone Soup**

Ingredients:

- 2 tablespoons olive oil
- 1 onion, diced
- 3 cloves garlic, minced
- 2 carrots, diced
- 2 celery stalks, diced
- 1 zucchini, diced
- 1 yellow squash, diced
- 1 bell pepper, diced
- 1 cup green beans, trimmed and cut into 1-inch pieces
- 1 can (14 oz) diced tomatoes
- 6 cups vegetable broth
- 1 can (15 oz) kidney beans, drained and rinsed
- 1 can (15 oz) cannellini beans, drained and rinsed
- 1 cup small pasta (such as elbow macaroni or small shells)
- 2 teaspoons dried Italian seasoning
- Salt and pepper to taste
- Fresh basil, chopped (for garnish)
- Grated Parmesan cheese (optional, for serving)

Instructions:

Saute Aromatics:

1. Heat olive oil in a large pot over medium heat. Add diced onion and minced garlic, and sauté until softened and fragrant, about 5 minutes.

Add Vegetables:

2. Add diced carrots, celery, zucchini, yellow squash, bell pepper, and green beans to the pot. Cook, stirring occasionally, for about 5-7 minutes, until the vegetables begin to soften.

Simmer Soup:

3. Pour in the diced tomatoes and vegetable broth. Bring the soup to a simmer.

Add Beans and Pasta:

4. Stir in the kidney beans, cannellini beans, and small pasta. Cook the soup at a gentle simmer for about 10-15 minutes, or until the pasta is cooked al dente and the vegetables are tender.

Season:

5. Stir in the dried Italian seasoning and season the soup with salt and pepper to taste. Adjust the seasoning as needed.

Serve:

6. Ladle the veggie-packed Minestrone Soup into bowls. Garnish each serving with chopped fresh basil and grated Parmesan cheese, if desired.

Enjoy!

7. Enjoy your warm and comforting Veggie-Packed Minestrone Soup as a nutritious meal.

Feel free to customize this recipe by adding any additional vegetables or herbs you prefer. Serve the soup with crusty bread or a side salad for a complete meal.

**Spinach and Feta Stuffed Chicken Breast**

Ingredients:

- 4 boneless, skinless chicken breasts
- 2 cups fresh spinach leaves
- 1/2 cup crumbled feta cheese
- 2 cloves garlic, minced
- 1 tablespoon olive oil
- 1/2 teaspoon dried oregano
- 1/2 teaspoon dried basil
- Salt and pepper to taste
- Toothpicks or kitchen twine

Instructions:

Preheat Oven:

1. Preheat your oven to 375°F (190°C).

Prepare Chicken Breasts:

2. Using a sharp knife, make a horizontal slit along the side of each chicken breast to form a pocket, being careful not to cut all the way through.

Prepare Filling:

3. In a skillet, heat olive oil over medium heat. Add minced garlic and cook for about 1 minute until fragrant. Add fresh spinach leaves and cook until wilted, about 2-3 minutes. Remove from heat and let it cool slightly. Once cooled, stir in crumbled feta cheese, dried oregano, dried basil, and season with salt and pepper.

Stuff Chicken Breasts:

4. Stuff each chicken breast pocket with the spinach and feta mixture, dividing it evenly among the breasts. Secure the openings with toothpicks or kitchen twine to hold the filling inside.

Season Chicken:

5. Season the outside of the stuffed chicken breasts with a little salt and pepper.

Cook Chicken:

6. Heat a large oven-safe skillet over medium-high heat. Add a little olive oil to the skillet, then add the stuffed chicken breasts. Cook for about 2-3 minutes on each side until they are golden brown.

Finish in Oven:

7. Transfer the skillet to the preheated oven and bake for 20-25 minutes, or until the chicken is cooked through and reaches an internal temperature of 165°F (75°C).

Serve:

8. Remove the toothpicks or kitchen twine from the chicken breasts before serving. Serve the Spinach and Feta Stuffed Chicken Breast hot, garnished with fresh herbs if desired.

Enjoy your flavorful and juicy Spinach and Feta Stuffed Chicken Breast!

**Thai Peanut Quinoa Bowl**

Ingredients:

For the Quinoa:

- 1 cup quinoa, rinsed
- 2 cups water or vegetable broth
- Pinch of salt

For the Peanut Sauce:

- 1/4 cup peanut butter
- 2 tablespoons soy sauce (or tamari for gluten-free)
- 1 tablespoon maple syrup or honey
- 1 tablespoon rice vinegar
- 1 clove garlic, minced
- 1 teaspoon grated fresh ginger
- 1 teaspoon sesame oil (optional)
- 2-4 tablespoons water, as needed to thin the sauce

For the Bowl:

- 1 cup shredded carrots
- 1 red bell pepper, thinly sliced
- 1 cucumber, thinly sliced
- 1 cup shredded purple cabbage
- 1 cup shelled edamame, cooked
- 1/4 cup chopped peanuts (for garnish)
- Fresh cilantro, chopped (for garnish)
- Lime wedges, for serving

Instructions:

Cook the Quinoa:

1. In a medium saucepan, combine the rinsed quinoa, water or vegetable broth, and a pinch of salt. Bring to a boil, then reduce the heat to low, cover, and simmer for 15-20 minutes, or until the quinoa is cooked and the liquid is absorbed. Remove from heat and let it sit, covered, for 5 minutes. Fluff with a fork and set aside.

Make the Peanut Sauce:

2. In a small bowl, whisk together peanut butter, soy sauce, maple syrup or honey, rice vinegar, minced garlic, grated ginger, and sesame oil (if using) until smooth. Add water, one tablespoon at a time, until the sauce reaches your desired consistency. Set aside.

Prepare the Bowl Ingredients:

3. Divide cooked quinoa among serving bowls. Arrange shredded carrots, thinly sliced red bell pepper, sliced cucumber, shredded purple cabbage, and cooked edamame on top of the quinoa.

Assemble the Bowls:

4. Drizzle each bowl with the prepared peanut sauce.

Garnish:

5. Garnish each bowl with chopped peanuts and fresh cilantro. Serve with lime wedges on the side.

Serve:

6. Serve the Thai Peanut Quinoa Bowls immediately and enjoy!

Feel free to customize your bowls by adding other toppings such as avocado slices, roasted tofu, or crispy fried shallots.

**Beef and Sweet Potato Stew**

Ingredients:

- 1 1/2 lbs beef stew meat, cut into bite-sized pieces
- 2 tablespoons olive oil
- 1 onion, chopped
- 3 cloves garlic, minced
- 2 medium sweet potatoes, peeled and diced
- 2 carrots, peeled and sliced
- 2 celery stalks, sliced
- 1 can (14.5 oz) diced tomatoes
- 4 cups beef broth
- 2 tablespoons tomato paste
- 1 teaspoon dried thyme
- 1 teaspoon dried rosemary
- Salt and pepper to taste
- Fresh parsley, chopped (for garnish)

Instructions:

Brown the Beef:

1. Heat 1 tablespoon of olive oil in a large pot or Dutch oven over medium-high heat. Add the beef stew meat in batches and brown on all sides, about 5 minutes per batch. Remove the browned beef from the pot and set aside.

Saute Aromatics:

2. In the same pot, add the remaining tablespoon of olive oil. Add chopped onion and minced garlic, and cook until softened, about 5 minutes.

Add Vegetables:

3. Add diced sweet potatoes, sliced carrots, and sliced celery to the pot. Cook for another 5 minutes, stirring occasionally.

Combine Ingredients:

4. Return the browned beef to the pot. Add diced tomatoes (with their juices), beef broth, tomato paste, dried thyme, and dried rosemary. Stir well to combine.

Simmer:

5. Bring the stew to a simmer. Reduce the heat to low, cover, and let it simmer for about 1 to 1 1/2 hours, stirring occasionally, or until the beef is tender and the sweet potatoes are cooked through.

Season:

6. Season the stew with salt and pepper to taste. Adjust the seasoning as needed.

Serve:

7. Ladle the Beef and Sweet Potato Stew into bowls. Garnish with chopped fresh parsley before serving.

Enjoy!

8. Enjoy your hearty and flavorful Beef and Sweet Potato Stew served hot. Serve with crusty bread or a side salad for a complete meal.

This stew is perfect for chilly days and makes great leftovers for lunch or dinner the next day.

**Mediterranean Baked Cod**

Ingredients:

- 4 cod fillets (about 6 oz each)
- 2 tablespoons olive oil
- 2 cloves garlic, minced
- 1 teaspoon dried oregano
- 1 teaspoon dried thyme
- 1 teaspoon dried rosemary
- 1/2 teaspoon paprika
- Salt and pepper to taste
- 1 lemon, thinly sliced
- 1/4 cup Kalamata olives, pitted and halved
- 1/4 cup cherry tomatoes, halved
- 2 tablespoons capers, drained
- Fresh parsley, chopped (for garnish)
- Lemon wedges (for serving)

Instructions:

Preheat Oven:

1. Preheat your oven to 400°F (200°C). Line a baking sheet with parchment paper or lightly grease it with olive oil.

Prepare the Cod:

2. Pat the cod fillets dry with paper towels and place them on the prepared baking sheet.

Season the Cod:

3. In a small bowl, combine olive oil, minced garlic, dried oregano, dried thyme, dried rosemary, paprika, salt, and pepper. Mix well to make a marinade. Brush the marinade over the cod fillets, coating them evenly.

Add Toppings:

4. Arrange lemon slices, halved cherry tomatoes, halved Kalamata olives, and capers on top of the cod fillets.

Bake:

5. Place the baking sheet in the preheated oven and bake for 12-15 minutes, or until the cod is opaque and flakes easily with a fork.

Garnish and Serve:

6. Remove the baked cod from the oven. Garnish with chopped fresh parsley and serve hot with lemon wedges on the side.

Enjoy!

7. Enjoy your flavorful Mediterranean Baked Cod as a delicious and healthy meal.

Serve the baked cod with your favorite sides, such as steamed vegetables, couscous, or a green salad, for a complete Mediterranean-inspired dinner.

**Zucchini Noodles with Pesto and Cherry Tomatoes**

Ingredients:

- 4 medium zucchini
- 1 cup cherry tomatoes, halved
- 1/4 cup prepared pesto sauce (store-bought or homemade)
- 2 tablespoons olive oil
- Salt and pepper to taste
- Grated Parmesan cheese (optional, for serving)
- Fresh basil leaves, chopped (for garnish)

Instructions:

Prepare Zucchini Noodles:

1. Use a spiralizer to spiralize the zucchini into noodles. Alternatively, you can use a julienne peeler or a mandoline slicer to create long, thin strips resembling noodles. Set the zucchini noodles aside.

Heat Olive Oil:

2. Heat olive oil in a large skillet over medium heat.

Cook Cherry Tomatoes:

3. Add the halved cherry tomatoes to the skillet and cook for 3-4 minutes, or until they start to soften and release their juices.

Add Zucchini Noodles:

4. Add the zucchini noodles to the skillet with the cherry tomatoes. Cook for 2-3 minutes, tossing gently, just until the zucchini noodles are heated through but still slightly crisp. Be careful not to overcook them, as they can become watery.

Toss with Pesto:

5. Add the prepared pesto sauce to the skillet with the zucchini noodles and cherry tomatoes. Toss everything together until the noodles are evenly coated with the pesto sauce.

Season:

6. Season with salt and pepper to taste. Remember that pesto sauce already contains salt, so be cautious with the additional salt.

Serve:

7. Divide the zucchini noodles with pesto and cherry tomatoes among serving plates. Optionally, sprinkle with grated Parmesan cheese and chopped fresh basil leaves for extra flavor and garnish.

Enjoy!

8. Enjoy your vibrant and flavorful Zucchini Noodles with Pesto and Cherry Tomatoes as a light and healthy meal.

This dish is perfect for a quick lunch or dinner and is a great way to enjoy the fresh flavors of summer produce.

**Cauliflower Rice Stir-Fry**

Ingredients:

- 1 medium head cauliflower, cut into florets
- 2 tablespoons sesame oil or vegetable oil
- 2 cloves garlic, minced
- 1 small onion, diced
- 1 carrot, diced
- 1 bell pepper, diced
- 1 cup broccoli florets
- 1 cup snap peas, trimmed
- 2 tablespoons soy sauce (or tamari for gluten-free)
- 1 tablespoon hoisin sauce
- 1 tablespoon rice vinegar
- 1 teaspoon sesame seeds (for garnish)
- Sliced green onions (for garnish)
- Salt and pepper to taste

Instructions:

Prepare Cauliflower Rice:

1. Place the cauliflower florets in a food processor and pulse until they resemble rice-like grains. Be careful not to over-process. Alternatively, you can use a box grater to grate the cauliflower into rice-like pieces.

Stir-Fry:

2. Heat sesame oil or vegetable oil in a large skillet or wok over medium-high heat. Add minced garlic and diced onion, and cook for 1-2 minutes until fragrant.

Add Vegetables:

3. Add diced carrot, diced bell pepper, broccoli florets, and snap peas to the skillet. Stir-fry for about 5 minutes, or until the vegetables are tender-crisp.

Cook Cauliflower Rice:

4. Push the vegetables to one side of the skillet and add the cauliflower rice to the empty space. Cook for 3-4 minutes, stirring occasionally, until the cauliflower rice is tender but not mushy.

Combine:

5. Stir the cooked vegetables into the cauliflower rice, mixing everything together evenly.

Add Sauces:

6. In a small bowl, mix together soy sauce, hoisin sauce, and rice vinegar. Pour the sauce mixture over the cauliflower rice and vegetables in the skillet. Stir well to coat everything with the sauce.

Season:

7. Season with salt and pepper to taste, if needed.

Garnish and Serve:

8. Garnish the Cauliflower Rice Stir-Fry with sesame seeds and sliced green onions.

Enjoy!

9. Serve hot and enjoy your flavorful and healthy Cauliflower Rice Stir-Fry as a delicious meal.

Feel free to customize this stir-fry with your favorite vegetables, protein (such as tofu, chicken, or shrimp), or additional seasonings to suit your taste preferences.

**Turkey and Quinoa Stuffed Bell Peppers**

Ingredients:

- 4 large bell peppers, any color
- 1 cup quinoa, rinsed
- 1 lb ground turkey
- 1 small onion, diced
- 2 cloves garlic, minced
- 1 can (14.5 oz) diced tomatoes, drained
- 1 cup tomato sauce
- 1 teaspoon dried oregano
- 1 teaspoon dried basil
- 1/2 teaspoon paprika
- Salt and pepper to taste
- 1 cup shredded mozzarella cheese (optional)
- Fresh parsley, chopped (for garnish)

Instructions:

Preheat Oven:

1. Preheat your oven to 375°F (190°C).

Prepare Bell Peppers:

2. Cut the tops off the bell peppers and remove the seeds and membranes from the inside. If needed, slice a small portion off the bottom of each pepper to help them stand upright in the baking dish. Place the prepared bell peppers in a baking dish and set aside.

Cook Quinoa:

3. In a medium saucepan, bring 2 cups of water to a boil. Add the rinsed quinoa, reduce heat to low, cover, and simmer for 15-20 minutes, or until the quinoa is cooked and the water is absorbed. Remove from heat and set aside.

Prepare Filling:

4. In a large skillet, cook the ground turkey over medium heat until browned and cooked through, breaking it up with a spoon as it cooks. Drain any excess fat.

Saute Aromatics:

5. Add diced onion and minced garlic to the skillet with the cooked turkey. Cook for 2-3 minutes until the onion is softened and translucent.

Combine Ingredients:

6. Stir in the drained diced tomatoes, tomato sauce, dried oregano, dried basil, paprika, cooked quinoa, salt, and pepper. Mix well to combine all the ingredients.

Stuff Bell Peppers:

7. Spoon the turkey and quinoa mixture evenly into the hollowed-out bell peppers, pressing gently to pack the filling.

Bake:

8. Cover the baking dish with aluminum foil and bake in the preheated oven for 25-30 minutes, or until the bell peppers are tender.

Add Cheese (Optional):

9. If using shredded mozzarella cheese, remove the foil from the baking dish and sprinkle the cheese over the stuffed bell peppers during the last 5 minutes of baking. Return to the oven until the cheese is melted and bubbly.

Garnish and Serve:

10. Remove the stuffed bell peppers from the oven and let them cool slightly. Garnish with chopped fresh parsley before serving.

Enjoy!

11. Serve the Turkey and Quinoa Stuffed Bell Peppers hot as a nutritious and satisfying meal.

Feel free to customize the filling with your favorite vegetables, herbs, or spices, and adjust the seasonings to suit your taste preferences.

**Shrimp and Avocado Salad**

Ingredients:

- 1 lb large shrimp, peeled and deveined
- 2 ripe avocados, diced
- 1 cup cherry tomatoes, halved
- 1/4 cup red onion, thinly sliced
- 1/4 cup fresh cilantro, chopped
- 2 tablespoons olive oil
- 2 tablespoons fresh lime juice
- 1 garlic clove, minced
- Salt and pepper to taste
- Mixed greens or lettuce leaves, for serving

Instructions:

Cook Shrimp:

1. Bring a large pot of salted water to a boil. Add the shrimp and cook until pink and opaque, about 2-3 minutes. Drain the shrimp and rinse under cold water to stop the cooking process. Pat dry with paper towels and set aside.

Prepare Dressing:

2. In a small bowl, whisk together olive oil, lime juice, minced garlic, salt, and pepper to make the dressing. Adjust seasoning to taste.

Assemble Salad:

3. In a large mixing bowl, combine the cooked shrimp, diced avocado, halved cherry tomatoes, thinly sliced red onion, and chopped fresh cilantro. Pour the dressing over the salad ingredients and gently toss until everything is evenly coated.

Serve:

4. Arrange mixed greens or lettuce leaves on serving plates or in a large salad bowl. Spoon the shrimp and avocado salad over the greens.

Garnish:

5. Garnish the salad with additional cilantro leaves and a sprinkle of black pepper, if desired.

Enjoy!

6. Serve the Shrimp and Avocado Salad immediately as a light and refreshing meal.

This salad is perfect for lunch or dinner and is packed with fresh flavors. You can also customize it by adding other ingredients like cucumber, bell peppers, or corn kernels.

**Hearty Lentil Soup**

Ingredients:

- 1 cup dry lentils (green or brown), rinsed and drained
- 1 onion, diced
- 2 carrots, diced
- 2 celery stalks, diced
- 3 cloves garlic, minced
- 1 can (14.5 oz) diced tomatoes
- 6 cups vegetable broth or chicken broth
- 1 teaspoon ground cumin
- 1 teaspoon ground coriander
- 1 teaspoon paprika
- 1/2 teaspoon dried thyme
- Salt and pepper to taste
- 2 tablespoons olive oil
- Fresh parsley, chopped (for garnish)
- Lemon wedges (for serving)
- Optional: chopped spinach or kale for extra greens

Instructions:

Saute Aromatics:

1. Heat olive oil in a large pot or Dutch oven over medium heat. Add diced onion, carrots, and celery. Cook, stirring occasionally, for about 5-7 minutes, or until the vegetables are softened.

Add Garlic and Spices:

2. Add minced garlic, ground cumin, ground coriander, paprika, and dried thyme to the pot. Stir well and cook for another 1-2 minutes until fragrant.

Add Lentils and Tomatoes:

3. Add rinsed and drained lentils and diced tomatoes (with their juices) to the pot. Stir to combine.

Pour in Broth:

4. Pour vegetable broth or chicken broth into the pot. Bring the soup to a boil, then reduce the heat to low and let it simmer, uncovered, for about 25-30 minutes, or until the lentils are tender.

Season:

5. Season the soup with salt and pepper to taste. Adjust seasoning as needed.

Optional Greens:

6. If desired, add chopped spinach or kale to the soup during the last 5 minutes of cooking. Stir until the greens are wilted.

Serve:

7. Ladle the hearty lentil soup into bowls. Garnish with chopped fresh parsley and serve with lemon wedges on the side.

Enjoy!

8. Enjoy your warm and comforting Hearty Lentil Soup as a satisfying meal.

This soup is perfect for chilly days and makes great leftovers for lunch or dinner the next day. Serve it with crusty bread or a side salad for a complete meal.

**Baked Lemon Herb Chicken**

Ingredients:

- 4 boneless, skinless chicken breasts
- 2 tablespoons olive oil
- 2 cloves garlic, minced
- Zest of 1 lemon
- Juice of 1 lemon
- 1 teaspoon dried thyme
- 1 teaspoon dried rosemary
- 1 teaspoon dried oregano
- Salt and pepper to taste
- Lemon slices (for garnish)
- Fresh parsley, chopped (for garnish)

Instructions:

Preheat Oven:

1. Preheat your oven to 400°F (200°C). Grease a baking dish or line it with parchment paper.

Prepare Chicken:

2. Pat the chicken breasts dry with paper towels. Place them in the prepared baking dish.

Make Marinade:

3. In a small bowl, whisk together olive oil, minced garlic, lemon zest, lemon juice, dried thyme, dried rosemary, dried oregano, salt, and pepper.

Marinate Chicken:

4. Pour the marinade over the chicken breasts, turning them to coat evenly. Let the chicken marinate for at least 20-30 minutes in the refrigerator, or longer for more flavor.

Bake Chicken:

5. Transfer the baking dish to the preheated oven and bake for 20-25 minutes, or until the chicken is cooked through and no longer pink in the center, or until it reaches an internal temperature of 165°F (75°C).

Baste (Optional):

6. If desired, baste the chicken with the juices from the bottom of the baking dish halfway through the cooking time for extra flavor and moisture.

Garnish and Serve:

7. Once the chicken is cooked, remove it from the oven. Garnish with lemon slices and chopped fresh parsley before serving.

Enjoy!

8. Serve the Baked Lemon Herb Chicken hot with your favorite sides, such as roasted vegetables, rice, or salad.

This Baked Lemon Herb Chicken is juicy, flavorful, and easy to make, making it perfect for a quick weeknight dinner or for entertaining guests.

**Quinoa and Veggie Stuffed Acorn Squash**

Ingredients:

- 2 acorn squash, halved and seeds removed
- 1 cup quinoa, rinsed
- 2 cups vegetable broth or water
- 1 tablespoon olive oil
- 1 onion, diced
- 2 cloves garlic, minced
- 1 bell pepper, diced (any color)
- 1 zucchini, diced
- 1 cup cherry tomatoes, halved
- 1 teaspoon dried thyme
- 1 teaspoon dried rosemary
- Salt and pepper to taste
- 1/4 cup grated Parmesan cheese (optional, for garnish)
- Fresh parsley, chopped (for garnish)

Instructions:

Preheat Oven:

1. Preheat your oven to 400°F (200°C).

Prepare Squash:

2. Cut the acorn squash in half lengthwise and scoop out the seeds and stringy pulp. Place the squash halves cut-side down on a baking sheet lined with parchment paper. Bake in the preheated oven for 30-35 minutes, or until the squash is tender when pierced with a fork.

Cook Quinoa:

3. While the squash is baking, combine the rinsed quinoa and vegetable broth or water in a saucepan. Bring to a boil, then reduce heat to low, cover, and simmer

for 15-20 minutes, or until the quinoa is cooked and the liquid is absorbed. Fluff with a fork and set aside.

Prepare Veggie Filling:

4. In a large skillet, heat olive oil over medium heat. Add diced onion and minced garlic, and cook until softened and fragrant, about 3-4 minutes.

Add Veggies and Herbs:

5. Add diced bell pepper, diced zucchini, halved cherry tomatoes, dried thyme, and dried rosemary to the skillet. Cook for 5-7 minutes, or until the vegetables are tender but still slightly crisp. Season with salt and pepper to taste.

Combine Quinoa and Veggie Filling:

6. Add the cooked quinoa to the skillet with the cooked vegetables. Stir well to combine all the ingredients.

Stuff Squash:

7. Flip the baked acorn squash halves over so they are cut-side up. Divide the quinoa and veggie mixture evenly among the squash halves, pressing down gently to pack the filling.

Bake Again:

8. Return the stuffed acorn squash to the oven and bake for an additional 10-15 minutes, or until heated through and the tops are slightly golden.

Garnish and Serve:

9. Remove the stuffed acorn squash from the oven. Garnish with grated Parmesan cheese (if using) and chopped fresh parsley before serving.

Enjoy!

10. Serve the Quinoa and Veggie Stuffed Acorn Squash hot as a nutritious and satisfying meal.

This dish is not only visually appealing but also packed with flavors and nutrients. It makes a great vegetarian main course or a hearty side dish for any meal.

**Spaghetti Squash with Marinara Sauce**

Ingredients:

- 1 medium spaghetti squash
- 2 cups marinara sauce (store-bought or homemade)
- Olive oil
- Salt and pepper to taste
- Grated Parmesan cheese (optional, for garnish)
- Fresh basil leaves, chopped (for garnish)

Instructions:

Prepare Spaghetti Squash:

1. Preheat your oven to 400°F (200°C). Cut the spaghetti squash in half lengthwise and scoop out the seeds and stringy pulp from the center. Drizzle the cut sides of the squash with olive oil and season with salt and pepper.

Bake Spaghetti Squash:

2. Place the spaghetti squash halves cut-side down on a baking sheet lined with parchment paper. Bake in the preheated oven for 30-40 minutes, or until the squash is tender when pierced with a fork.

Scrape Flesh:

3. Remove the spaghetti squash from the oven and let it cool slightly. Use a fork to scrape the flesh of the squash into spaghetti-like strands. Place the strands in a serving bowl.

Heat Marinara Sauce:

4. Meanwhile, heat the marinara sauce in a saucepan over medium heat until warmed through. You can use store-bought marinara sauce or homemade marinara sauce.

Serve:

5. Pour the warm marinara sauce over the spaghetti squash strands. Toss gently to coat the squash evenly with the sauce.

Garnish and Serve:

6. Garnish the spaghetti squash with grated Parmesan cheese (if using) and chopped fresh basil leaves. Serve hot.

Enjoy!

7. Enjoy your Spaghetti Squash with Marinara Sauce as a nutritious and satisfying meal.

This dish is a healthy and low-carb alternative to traditional pasta dishes, and it's packed with flavor. You can also customize it by adding other toppings such as sautéed vegetables, cooked shrimp, or shredded chicken.

**Seared Tuna with Mango Salsa**

Ingredients:

- 4 tuna steaks (about 6 oz each), preferably sushi-grade
- 2 tablespoons soy sauce
- 1 tablespoon sesame oil
- 1 tablespoon olive oil
- Salt and pepper to taste
- For the Mango Salsa:
    - 1 ripe mango, peeled and diced
    - 1/2 red onion, finely chopped
    - 1 red bell pepper, diced
    - 1 jalapeño pepper, seeded and minced
    - 1/4 cup fresh cilantro, chopped
    - Juice of 1 lime
    - Salt and pepper to taste

Instructions:

Prepare Mango Salsa:

1. In a medium bowl, combine diced mango, finely chopped red onion, diced red bell pepper, minced jalapeño pepper, chopped fresh cilantro, and lime juice. Season with salt and pepper to taste. Mix well and set aside to allow the flavors to meld.

Marinate Tuna:

2. In a shallow dish, whisk together soy sauce and sesame oil. Place the tuna steaks in the marinade, turning to coat evenly. Let the tuna marinate for about 15-30 minutes in the refrigerator.

Season Tuna:

3. Remove the tuna steaks from the marinade and pat them dry with paper towels. Season both sides of the tuna steaks with salt and pepper.

Heat Oil:

4. Heat olive oil in a large skillet or grill pan over high heat until hot but not smoking.

Sear Tuna:

5. Carefully add the tuna steaks to the hot skillet. Cook for about 1-2 minutes on each side for rare to medium-rare, depending on the thickness of the steaks, or cook to your desired level of doneness.

Rest:

6. Remove the seared tuna steaks from the skillet and let them rest for a few minutes before slicing.

Slice and Serve:

7. Slice the seared tuna steaks thinly against the grain. Arrange the sliced tuna on serving plates and top with mango salsa.

Garnish and Serve:

8. Garnish the Seared Tuna with Mango Salsa with additional fresh cilantro leaves, if desired. Serve immediately.

Enjoy!

9. Enjoy your flavorful and vibrant Seared Tuna with Mango Salsa as a light and refreshing meal.

This dish is perfect for a special dinner or a light lunch, and it's sure to impress with its beautiful presentation and delicious flavors.

**Black Bean and Corn Salad**

Ingredients:

- 2 cups cooked black beans (or 1 can, drained and rinsed)
- 1 1/2 cups corn kernels (fresh, frozen, or canned)
- 1 red bell pepper, diced
- 1/2 red onion, finely chopped
- 1 jalapeño pepper, seeded and minced (optional)
- 1/4 cup fresh cilantro, chopped
- 2 tablespoons lime juice
- 2 tablespoons olive oil
- 1 teaspoon ground cumin
- 1/2 teaspoon chili powder
- Salt and pepper to taste
- Avocado, diced (optional, for serving)
- Tortilla chips or lettuce leaves (for serving)

Instructions:

Prepare Ingredients:

1. If using canned black beans, drain and rinse them under cold water. If using fresh corn, cook or grill the corn until tender, then cut the kernels off the cob. If using frozen corn, thaw it by running it under cold water.

Combine Ingredients:

2. In a large mixing bowl, combine the cooked black beans, corn kernels, diced red bell pepper, finely chopped red onion, minced jalapeño pepper (if using), and chopped fresh cilantro.

Make Dressing:

3. In a small bowl, whisk together lime juice, olive oil, ground cumin, chili powder, salt, and pepper to make the dressing.

Dress Salad:

4. Pour the dressing over the black bean and corn mixture. Toss everything together until well combined and evenly coated with the dressing.

Chill (Optional):

5. For best flavor, refrigerate the salad for at least 30 minutes to allow the flavors to meld together. However, you can also serve it immediately if you're short on time.

Serve:

6. Serve the Black Bean and Corn Salad as a side dish or as a main course. You can serve it on its own, with diced avocado on top, or as a topping for tortilla chips or lettuce leaves.

Enjoy!

7. Enjoy your fresh and flavorful Black Bean and Corn Salad as a delicious and nutritious dish.

This salad is perfect for summer gatherings, potlucks, or as a side dish for grilled meats. It's also great for meal prep and can be stored in the refrigerator for a few days.

**Chicken and Wild Rice Soup**

Ingredients:

- 1 cup wild rice blend
- 1 lb boneless, skinless chicken breasts, diced
- 1 tablespoon olive oil
- 1 onion, diced
- 2 carrots, diced
- 2 celery stalks, diced
- 3 cloves garlic, minced
- 8 cups chicken broth
- 1 teaspoon dried thyme
- 1 teaspoon dried rosemary
- 1 bay leaf
- Salt and pepper to taste
- 1/2 cup heavy cream or half-and-half (optional)
- Fresh parsley, chopped (for garnish)

Instructions:

Cook Wild Rice:

1. Cook the wild rice blend according to the package instructions. Drain any excess water and set aside.

Cook Chicken:

2. In a large pot or Dutch oven, heat olive oil over medium heat. Add diced chicken breasts and cook until browned on all sides, about 5-6 minutes. Remove the chicken from the pot and set aside.

Saute Aromatics:

3. In the same pot, add diced onion, carrots, and celery. Cook until softened, about 5 minutes. Add minced garlic and cook for an additional 1 minute until fragrant.

Add Broth and Seasonings:

4. Pour in the chicken broth and return the cooked chicken to the pot. Add dried thyme, dried rosemary, bay leaf, salt, and pepper. Stir to combine.

Simmer:

5. Bring the soup to a simmer. Reduce heat to low, cover, and let it simmer for 20-25 minutes, or until the vegetables are tender and the flavors are well blended.

Add Cooked Rice:

6. Add the cooked wild rice blend to the soup and stir well to combine. If using, stir in the heavy cream or half-and-half to add richness to the soup. Cook for an additional 5 minutes to heat through.

Adjust Seasoning:

7. Taste the soup and adjust the seasoning with more salt and pepper if needed, according to your taste preferences.

Serve:

8. Ladle the Chicken and Wild Rice Soup into bowls. Garnish with chopped fresh parsley before serving.

Enjoy!

9. Serve the soup hot as a comforting and satisfying meal.

This Chicken and Wild Rice Soup is hearty, flavorful, and perfect for warming up on cold days. Serve it with crusty bread or a side salad for a complete meal.

**Grilled Veggie and Quinoa Bowl**

Ingredients:

- 1 cup quinoa, rinsed
- 2 cups vegetable broth or water
- 2 zucchinis, sliced lengthwise
- 2 bell peppers, seeded and quartered
- 1 red onion, sliced into thick rounds
- 1 cup cherry tomatoes
- 1/4 cup balsamic vinegar
- 2 tablespoons olive oil
- 2 cloves garlic, minced
- Salt and pepper to taste
- Fresh herbs (such as parsley or basil), chopped for garnish

Instructions:

Cook Quinoa:

1. In a medium saucepan, bring vegetable broth or water to a boil. Add the rinsed quinoa, reduce heat to low, cover, and simmer for 15-20 minutes, or until the quinoa is cooked and the liquid is absorbed. Fluff with a fork and set aside.

Prepare Grill:

2. Preheat your grill to medium-high heat.

Marinate Veggies:

3. In a large bowl, whisk together balsamic vinegar, olive oil, minced garlic, salt, and pepper. Add the sliced zucchinis, quartered bell peppers, sliced red onion, and cherry tomatoes to the bowl. Toss to coat the vegetables evenly with the marinade.

Grill Veggies:

4. Place the marinated vegetables on the preheated grill. Grill for 5-7 minutes per side, or until the vegetables are tender and lightly charred. Remove from the grill and set aside.

Assemble Bowls:

5. Divide the cooked quinoa among serving bowls. Top with the grilled vegetables.

Garnish and Serve:

6. Garnish the Grilled Veggie and Quinoa Bowls with chopped fresh herbs, such as parsley or basil. Drizzle any remaining marinade over the bowls if desired.

Enjoy!

7. Serve the Grilled Veggie and Quinoa Bowls hot as a nutritious and satisfying meal.

This dish is versatile and customizable, so feel free to add your favorite grilled vegetables or adjust the marinade to suit your taste preferences. It's perfect for a light lunch or dinner and is packed with flavor and wholesome ingredients.

**Mushroom and Barley Soup**

Ingredients:

- 1 cup pearl barley, rinsed
- 8 cups vegetable broth or chicken broth
- 2 tablespoons olive oil
- 1 onion, diced
- 3 cloves garlic, minced
- 1 lb mushrooms (such as cremini or button), sliced
- 2 carrots, diced
- 2 celery stalks, diced
- 1 teaspoon dried thyme
- 1 teaspoon dried rosemary
- Salt and pepper to taste
- Fresh parsley, chopped (for garnish)

Instructions:

Cook Barley:

1. In a large pot, bring the vegetable broth or chicken broth to a boil. Add the rinsed pearl barley and reduce heat to low. Simmer, covered, for about 30-40 minutes, or until the barley is tender and cooked through. Drain any excess liquid and set aside.

Saute Aromatics:

2. In the same pot, heat olive oil over medium heat. Add diced onion and minced garlic. Cook until softened and fragrant, about 5 minutes.

Add Mushrooms and Veggies:

3. Add sliced mushrooms, diced carrots, and diced celery to the pot. Cook, stirring occasionally, until the vegetables are tender, about 8-10 minutes.

Season Soup:

4. Stir in dried thyme, dried rosemary, salt, and pepper to taste. Cook for an additional 1-2 minutes to allow the flavors to meld together.

Combine Barley and Veggies:

5. Add the cooked barley to the pot with the vegetables. Stir well to combine all the ingredients.

Simmer:

6. Let the soup simmer for another 10-15 minutes to allow the flavors to develop further.

Adjust Seasoning:

7. Taste the soup and adjust the seasoning with more salt and pepper if needed.

Serve:

8. Ladle the Mushroom and Barley Soup into bowls. Garnish with chopped fresh parsley before serving.

Enjoy!

9. Serve the soup hot as a comforting and satisfying meal.

This Mushroom and Barley Soup is hearty, nutritious, and perfect for chilly days. It's packed with earthy flavors from the mushrooms and barley, making it a comforting option for lunch or dinner.

**Chickpea and Spinach Stew**

Ingredients:

- 2 tablespoons olive oil
- 1 onion, finely chopped
- 3 cloves garlic, minced
- 1 teaspoon ground cumin
- 1 teaspoon ground coriander
- 1/2 teaspoon smoked paprika
- 1/4 teaspoon cayenne pepper (optional, for heat)
- 1 can (15 oz) chickpeas, drained and rinsed
- 1 can (14.5 oz) diced tomatoes
- 3 cups vegetable broth
- 4 cups fresh spinach leaves
- Salt and pepper to taste
- Fresh parsley or cilantro, chopped (for garnish)
- Lemon wedges (for serving)
- Cooked rice or crusty bread (for serving)

Instructions:

Saute Aromatics:

1. Heat olive oil in a large pot over medium heat. Add chopped onion and cook until softened, about 5 minutes. Add minced garlic and cook for another 1-2 minutes until fragrant.

Add Spices:

2. Stir in ground cumin, ground coriander, smoked paprika, and cayenne pepper (if using). Cook for a minute until the spices are toasted and fragrant.

Add Chickpeas and Tomatoes:

3. Add drained and rinsed chickpeas and diced tomatoes (with their juices) to the pot. Stir well to combine all the ingredients.

Pour in Broth:

4. Pour vegetable broth into the pot and bring the mixture to a simmer. Let it cook for about 10 minutes to allow the flavors to meld together.

Add Spinach:

5. Stir in fresh spinach leaves and cook until wilted, about 3-5 minutes.

Season:

6. Taste the stew and season with salt and pepper to taste. Adjust seasoning as needed.

Serve:

7. Ladle the Chickpea and Spinach Stew into bowls. Garnish with chopped fresh parsley or cilantro. Serve with lemon wedges on the side for squeezing over the stew. Serve with cooked rice or crusty bread for a complete meal.

Enjoy!

8. Serve the stew hot and enjoy its comforting and nutritious flavors.

This Chickpea and Spinach Stew is packed with protein, fiber, and vitamins, making it a hearty and satisfying vegetarian meal. It's perfect for a cozy dinner or for meal prep to enjoy throughout the week.

**Almond-Crusted Baked Chicken**

Ingredients:

- 4 boneless, skinless chicken breasts
- 1 cup almond flour
- 1/2 cup finely chopped almonds
- 1 teaspoon garlic powder
- 1 teaspoon paprika
- 1/2 teaspoon salt
- 1/4 teaspoon black pepper
- 2 eggs, beaten
- Cooking spray or olive oil

Instructions:

Preheat Oven:

1. Preheat your oven to 400°F (200°C). Line a baking sheet with parchment paper or lightly grease it with cooking spray or olive oil.

Prepare Chicken:

2. Place each chicken breast between two sheets of plastic wrap or parchment paper. Use a meat mallet or rolling pin to pound the chicken to an even thickness, about 1/2 inch thick.

Prepare Breading Station:

3. In one shallow bowl, place beaten eggs. In another shallow bowl, combine almond flour, finely chopped almonds, garlic powder, paprika, salt, and black pepper. Mix well to combine.

Coat Chicken:

4. Dip each chicken breast into the beaten eggs, allowing any excess to drip off. Then, dredge the chicken in the almond flour mixture, pressing gently to adhere the coating to both sides of the chicken.

Arrange on Baking Sheet:

5. Place the breaded chicken breasts on the prepared baking sheet, leaving space between each piece.

Bake:

6. Lightly spray the top of each chicken breast with cooking spray or drizzle with a little olive oil. Bake in the preheated oven for 20-25 minutes, or until the chicken is cooked through and the coating is golden brown and crispy.

Serve:

7. Remove the Almond-Crusted Baked Chicken from the oven and let it rest for a few minutes before serving.

Enjoy!

8. Serve the chicken hot as a delicious and nutritious main course. It pairs well with your favorite side dishes, such as roasted vegetables, salad, or quinoa.

This Almond-Crusted Baked Chicken is crispy on the outside, juicy on the inside, and packed with flavor. It's a healthier alternative to traditional fried chicken and makes for a satisfying meal that the whole family will love.

**Sweet Potato and Black Bean Tacos**

Ingredients:

- 2 medium sweet potatoes, peeled and diced
- 1 tablespoon olive oil
- 1 teaspoon ground cumin
- 1 teaspoon chili powder
- 1/2 teaspoon smoked paprika
- Salt and pepper to taste
- 1 can (15 oz) black beans, drained and rinsed
- 1 cup corn kernels (fresh, frozen, or canned)
- 1/2 red onion, diced
- 2 cloves garlic, minced
- 1 lime, juiced
- 8 small corn or flour tortillas
- Toppings: sliced avocado, chopped cilantro, salsa, lime wedges, etc.

Instructions:

Roast Sweet Potatoes:

1. Preheat your oven to 400°F (200°C). Place diced sweet potatoes on a baking sheet. Drizzle with olive oil and sprinkle with ground cumin, chili powder, smoked paprika, salt, and pepper. Toss to coat evenly. Roast in the preheated oven for 20-25 minutes, or until the sweet potatoes are tender and lightly browned.

Prepare Black Bean Mixture:

2. While the sweet potatoes are roasting, heat olive oil in a skillet over medium heat. Add diced red onion and minced garlic. Cook until softened, about 5 minutes. Add black beans and corn kernels to the skillet. Cook until heated through, about 3-5 minutes. Squeeze lime juice over the mixture and stir to combine. Season with salt and pepper to taste.

Warm Tortillas:

3. Warm tortillas according to package instructions. You can heat them in a dry skillet or wrap them in aluminum foil and warm them in the oven for a few minutes.

Assemble Tacos:

4. Fill each warmed tortilla with roasted sweet potatoes and the black bean mixture.

Add Toppings:

5. Top the tacos with your favorite toppings, such as sliced avocado, chopped cilantro, salsa, or a squeeze of lime juice.

Serve:

6. Serve the Sweet Potato and Black Bean Tacos immediately, and enjoy!

These tacos are packed with flavor, protein, and nutrients, making them a delicious and satisfying meal for lunch or dinner. Feel free to customize them with your favorite toppings and serve alongside rice, salad, or a side of chips and guacamole.

**Garlic Shrimp and Broccoli**

Ingredients:

- 1 lb large shrimp, peeled and deveined
- 3 cups broccoli florets
- 4 cloves garlic, minced
- 2 tablespoons olive oil
- 1 tablespoon soy sauce
- 1 tablespoon lemon juice
- Salt and pepper to taste
- Red pepper flakes (optional, for heat)
- Cooked rice or noodles, for serving

Instructions:

Prepare Shrimp:

1. Pat the shrimp dry with paper towels and season with salt and pepper.

Steam Broccoli:

2. In a pot fitted with a steamer basket, bring water to a boil. Add broccoli florets to the steamer basket and steam for about 3-4 minutes, or until the broccoli is tender but still crisp. Remove from heat and set aside.

Cook Shrimp:

3. Heat olive oil in a large skillet over medium-high heat. Add minced garlic and cook for about 1 minute until fragrant. Add the seasoned shrimp to the skillet and cook for 2-3 minutes per side, or until the shrimp turn pink and opaque.

Combine:

4. Add steamed broccoli florets to the skillet with the cooked shrimp. Drizzle soy sauce and lemon juice over the shrimp and broccoli. Toss everything together to coat evenly. If desired, sprinkle with red pepper flakes for added heat.

Serve:

5. Serve the Garlic Shrimp and Broccoli hot over cooked rice or noodles.

Enjoy!

6. Enjoy this delicious and nutritious dish as a quick and satisfying meal.

This Garlic Shrimp and Broccoli dish is not only easy to make but also packed with flavor and nutrients. It's perfect for busy weeknights when you want a healthy meal on the table in no time.

**Vegan Buddha Bowl**

Ingredients:

For the Bowl:

- 1 cup quinoa, rinsed
- 2 cups vegetable broth or water
- 1 tablespoon olive oil
- 1 large sweet potato, peeled and cubed
- 1 bunch broccoli, cut into florets
- 1 can (15 oz) chickpeas, drained and rinsed
- Salt and pepper to taste
- Optional toppings: avocado slices, sliced cucumber, shredded carrots, sliced radishes, cherry tomatoes, etc.

For the Tahini Dressing:

- 1/4 cup tahini
- 2 tablespoons lemon juice
- 2 tablespoons water
- 1 clove garlic, minced
- 1 teaspoon maple syrup or agave syrup
- Salt and pepper to taste

Instructions:

Cook Quinoa:

1. In a medium saucepan, bring vegetable broth or water to a boil. Add the rinsed quinoa, reduce heat to low, cover, and simmer for 15-20 minutes, or until the quinoa is cooked and the liquid is absorbed. Fluff with a fork and set aside.

Roast Veggies:

2. Preheat your oven to 400°F (200°C). Place cubed sweet potatoes, broccoli florets, and chickpeas on a baking sheet. Drizzle with olive oil and season with salt and pepper. Toss to coat evenly. Roast in the preheated oven for 20-25 minutes, or until the vegetables are tender and lightly browned.

Prepare Tahini Dressing:

3. In a small bowl, whisk together tahini, lemon juice, water, minced garlic, maple syrup, salt, and pepper until smooth and creamy. Adjust the consistency with more water if needed.

Assemble Buddha Bowls:

4. Divide cooked quinoa among serving bowls. Arrange roasted sweet potatoes, broccoli, and chickpeas on top of the quinoa. Add any optional toppings of your choice, such as avocado slices, sliced cucumber, shredded carrots, sliced radishes, cherry tomatoes, etc.

Drizzle with Dressing:

5. Drizzle Tahini Dressing over the Buddha Bowls just before serving.

Enjoy!

6. Enjoy your Vegan Buddha Bowls as a nourishing and satisfying meal.

These Vegan Buddha Bowls are not only visually appealing but also packed with flavor, protein, and nutrients. They are versatile, customizable, and perfect for meal prep. Feel free to mix and match the veggies and toppings according to your preferences.

**Greek Chicken and Vegetable Skewers**

Ingredients:

For the Marinade:

- 1/4 cup olive oil
- 3 tablespoons lemon juice
- 2 cloves garlic, minced
- 1 teaspoon dried oregano
- 1/2 teaspoon dried thyme
- 1/2 teaspoon dried rosemary
- Salt and pepper to taste

For the Skewers:

- 1 lb boneless, skinless chicken breasts, cut into cubes
- 1 red bell pepper, cut into chunks
- 1 yellow bell pepper, cut into chunks
- 1 red onion, cut into chunks
- Cherry tomatoes
- Wooden skewers, soaked in water for 30 minutes

Instructions:

Prepare Marinade:

1. In a small bowl, whisk together olive oil, lemon juice, minced garlic, dried oregano, dried thyme, dried rosemary, salt, and pepper to make the marinade.

Marinate Chicken:

2. Place the cubed chicken breasts in a shallow dish or resealable plastic bag. Pour the marinade over the chicken, making sure it's evenly coated. Cover the dish or

seal the bag and refrigerate for at least 30 minutes, or up to 4 hours, to allow the flavors to meld together.

Prepare Skewers:

3. Preheat your grill or grill pan to medium-high heat. Thread marinated chicken cubes, bell pepper chunks, red onion chunks, and cherry tomatoes onto the soaked wooden skewers, alternating between the ingredients.

Grill Skewers:

4. Lightly oil the grill grates or grill pan. Place the assembled skewers on the grill and cook for 8-10 minutes, turning occasionally, until the chicken is cooked through and the vegetables are tender and lightly charred.

Serve:

5. Remove the Greek Chicken and Vegetable Skewers from the grill and transfer them to a serving platter.

Enjoy!

6. Serve the skewers hot as a delicious and flavorful meal. Optionally, serve with a side of tzatziki sauce, Greek salad, or pita bread.

These Greek Chicken and Vegetable Skewers are bursting with Mediterranean flavors and are perfect for a summer barbecue or weeknight dinner. They're easy to make, healthy, and sure to be a hit with family and friends.

**Stuffed Portobello Mushrooms**

Ingredients:

- 4 large portobello mushrooms
- 1 tablespoon olive oil
- 2 cloves garlic, minced
- 1/2 onion, finely chopped
- 1 red bell pepper, finely chopped
- 1 cup baby spinach, chopped
- 1/2 cup breadcrumbs
- 1/2 cup grated Parmesan cheese
- 1/4 cup chopped fresh parsley
- Salt and pepper to taste
- Optional toppings: additional grated Parmesan cheese, chopped fresh parsley, red pepper flakes

Instructions:

Preheat Oven:

1. Preheat your oven to 375°F (190°C).

Prepare Mushrooms:

2. Clean the portobello mushrooms and remove the stems. Use a spoon to gently scrape out the gills from the mushroom caps and discard them.

Prepare Filling:

3. In a skillet, heat olive oil over medium heat. Add minced garlic and chopped onion, and cook until softened, about 3-4 minutes. Add chopped red bell pepper and cook for another 2-3 minutes. Stir in chopped baby spinach and cook until wilted, about 1-2 minutes. Remove from heat.

Make Stuffing:

4. In a mixing bowl, combine the cooked vegetable mixture with breadcrumbs, grated Parmesan cheese, chopped fresh parsley, salt, and pepper. Mix until well combined.

Stuff Mushrooms:

5. Place the portobello mushroom caps on a baking sheet lined with parchment paper. Fill each mushroom cap with the stuffing mixture, pressing down gently to pack it in.

Bake:

6. Bake the stuffed portobello mushrooms in the preheated oven for 20-25 minutes, or until the mushrooms are tender and the stuffing is golden brown and crispy on top.

Serve:

7. Remove the stuffed portobello mushrooms from the oven and let them cool slightly before serving.

Enjoy!

8. Serve the Stuffed Portobello Mushrooms hot as a delicious appetizer or main dish. Optionally, garnish with additional grated Parmesan cheese, chopped fresh parsley, or red pepper flakes before serving.

These Stuffed Portobello Mushrooms are hearty, flavorful, and perfect for vegetarians and mushroom lovers alike. They make a satisfying meal or appetizer that's sure to impress your guests. Feel free to customize the filling with your favorite ingredients or add a sprinkle of red pepper flakes for extra heat.

**Cabbage and Beef Soup**

Ingredients:

- 1 lb lean ground beef
- 1 tablespoon olive oil
- 1 onion, diced
- 3 cloves garlic, minced
- 4 cups beef broth
- 2 cups water
- 1 can (14.5 oz) diced tomatoes
- 1 small head cabbage, chopped
- 2 carrots, diced
- 2 celery stalks, diced
- 2 teaspoons dried thyme
- 1 teaspoon dried oregano
- Salt and pepper to taste
- Fresh parsley, chopped (for garnish)

Instructions:

Brown Ground Beef:

1. In a large pot or Dutch oven, heat olive oil over medium heat. Add lean ground beef and cook until browned, breaking it apart with a spoon as it cooks. Drain any excess fat if necessary.

Saute Aromatics:

2. Add diced onion and minced garlic to the pot with the cooked ground beef. Cook until the onions are softened and translucent, about 5 minutes.

Add Broth and Tomatoes:

3. Pour beef broth and water into the pot. Add diced tomatoes (with their juices) to the pot as well. Stir to combine.

Add Vegetables and Seasonings:

4. Add chopped cabbage, diced carrots, diced celery, dried thyme, and dried oregano to the pot. Season with salt and pepper to taste. Stir well to combine all the ingredients.

Simmer:

5. Bring the soup to a simmer. Reduce heat to low, cover, and let it simmer for about 20-25 minutes, or until the vegetables are tender and the flavors are well blended.

Adjust Seasoning:

6. Taste the soup and adjust the seasoning with more salt and pepper if needed.

Serve:

7. Ladle the Cabbage and Beef Soup into bowls. Garnish with chopped fresh parsley before serving.

Enjoy!

8. Serve the soup hot as a comforting and satisfying meal.

This Cabbage and Beef Soup is hearty, nutritious, and perfect for warming up on cold days. It's packed with vegetables and flavorful spices, making it a delicious and satisfying option for lunch or dinner. Serve it with crusty bread or a side salad for a complete meal.

**Roasted Cauliflower and Chickpea Tacos**

Ingredients:

For the Roasted Cauliflower and Chickpeas:

- 1 head cauliflower, cut into small florets
- 1 can (15 oz) chickpeas, drained and rinsed
- 2 tablespoons olive oil
- 1 teaspoon chili powder
- 1 teaspoon ground cumin
- 1/2 teaspoon smoked paprika
- Salt and pepper to taste

For the Tacos:

- 8 small corn or flour tortillas
- 1 avocado, sliced
- 1/2 cup shredded red cabbage
- 1/4 cup chopped fresh cilantro
- Lime wedges for serving

For the Creamy Avocado Sauce:

- 1 ripe avocado
- 1/4 cup plain Greek yogurt (or dairy-free yogurt for vegan option)
- 2 tablespoons lime juice
- 1 clove garlic, minced
- Salt and pepper to taste
- Water (as needed to thin out the sauce)

Instructions:

Preheat Oven:

1. Preheat your oven to 425°F (220°C) and line a baking sheet with parchment paper.

Prepare Cauliflower and Chickpeas:

2. In a large bowl, toss cauliflower florets and chickpeas with olive oil, chili powder, cumin, smoked paprika, salt, and pepper until evenly coated. Spread the mixture onto the prepared baking sheet in a single layer.

Roast:

3. Roast the cauliflower and chickpeas in the preheated oven for 20-25 minutes, or until the cauliflower is tender and lightly browned, and the chickpeas are crispy.

Make Creamy Avocado Sauce:

4. While the cauliflower and chickpeas are roasting, prepare the creamy avocado sauce. In a blender or food processor, combine ripe avocado, Greek yogurt, lime juice, minced garlic, salt, and pepper. Blend until smooth and creamy. If the sauce is too thick, add a little water to thin it out to your desired consistency.

Assemble Tacos:

5. Warm the tortillas according to package instructions. Spread a spoonful of creamy avocado sauce onto each tortilla. Top with roasted cauliflower and chickpeas, sliced avocado, shredded red cabbage, and chopped cilantro.

Serve:

6. Serve the Roasted Cauliflower and Chickpea Tacos with lime wedges on the side for squeezing over the tacos.

Enjoy!

7. Enjoy these delicious and flavorful tacos as a satisfying meatless meal.

These Roasted Cauliflower and Chickpea Tacos are loaded with flavor and texture, making them a perfect option for a plant-based dinner. The creamy avocado sauce adds a delightful creaminess to the tacos, while the roasted cauliflower and chickpeas provide a satisfying crunch. Serve them with your favorite toppings and enjoy!

## Chicken and Avocado Salad

Ingredients:

- 2 boneless, skinless chicken breasts
- 1 avocado, diced
- 1/2 cup cherry tomatoes, halved
- 1/4 cup red onion, finely chopped
- 2 tablespoons fresh cilantro or parsley, chopped
- 1 tablespoon olive oil
- 1 tablespoon lime juice
- Salt and pepper to taste
- Optional: mixed greens or lettuce leaves for serving

Instructions:

Cook Chicken:

1. Season the chicken breasts with salt and pepper. Heat olive oil in a skillet over medium-high heat. Add the chicken breasts and cook for 6-7 minutes per side, or until cooked through and no longer pink in the center. Remove from heat and let cool slightly.

Prepare Salad Ingredients:

2. While the chicken is cooking, prepare the salad ingredients. Dice the avocado, halve the cherry tomatoes, finely chop the red onion, and chop the fresh cilantro or parsley. Place them all in a large mixing bowl.

Slice Chicken:

3. Once the chicken has cooled slightly, slice it into thin strips or cubes.

Assemble Salad:

4. Add the sliced chicken to the mixing bowl with the salad ingredients.

Make Dressing:

5. In a small bowl, whisk together olive oil and lime juice to make the dressing. Season with salt and pepper to taste.

Toss Salad:

6. Drizzle the dressing over the salad ingredients in the mixing bowl. Gently toss everything together until well combined and evenly coated with the dressing.

Serve:

7. If desired, serve the Chicken and Avocado Salad over a bed of mixed greens or lettuce leaves.

Enjoy!

8. Serve the salad immediately as a delicious and satisfying meal.

This Chicken and Avocado Salad is light, refreshing, and packed with flavor. It's perfect for a quick and easy lunch or dinner and can be customized with your favorite salad toppings or additional veggies. Enjoy!

**Spinach and Quinoa Stuffed Bell Peppers**

Ingredients:

- 4 large bell peppers (any color), tops cut off and seeds removed
- 1 cup quinoa, rinsed
- 2 cups vegetable broth or water
- 1 tablespoon olive oil
- 1 onion, diced
- 2 cloves garlic, minced
- 2 cups fresh spinach leaves, chopped
- 1 can (15 oz) black beans, drained and rinsed
- 1 can (14.5 oz) diced tomatoes, drained
- 1 teaspoon ground cumin
- 1 teaspoon paprika
- Salt and pepper to taste
- 1 cup shredded cheese (cheddar, mozzarella, or your choice)
- Optional toppings: chopped fresh cilantro, avocado slices, sour cream, salsa

Instructions:

Preheat Oven:

1. Preheat your oven to 375°F (190°C). Lightly grease a baking dish large enough to hold the bell peppers upright.

Cook Quinoa:

2. In a medium saucepan, bring vegetable broth or water to a boil. Add the rinsed quinoa, reduce heat to low, cover, and simmer for 15-20 minutes, or until the quinoa is cooked and the liquid is absorbed. Fluff with a fork and set aside.

Prepare Bell Peppers:

3. Place the hollowed-out bell peppers in the prepared baking dish. If needed, trim the bottoms slightly to help them stand upright.

Make Filling:

4. In a large skillet, heat olive oil over medium heat. Add diced onion and minced garlic. Cook until softened, about 5 minutes. Add chopped spinach and cook until wilted, about 2-3 minutes.

Assemble Filling:

5. Add cooked quinoa, black beans, diced tomatoes, ground cumin, paprika, salt, and pepper to the skillet with the cooked onion and spinach. Stir well to combine all the ingredients. Cook for an additional 2-3 minutes, allowing the flavors to meld together.

Stuff Bell Peppers:

6. Spoon the quinoa and spinach mixture evenly into the hollowed-out bell peppers, pressing down gently to pack the filling.

Bake:

7. Sprinkle shredded cheese over the top of each stuffed bell pepper. Cover the baking dish with aluminum foil and bake in the preheated oven for 25-30 minutes, or until the bell peppers are tender and the cheese is melted and bubbly.

Serve:

8. Remove the stuffed bell peppers from the oven and let them cool slightly before serving.

Enjoy!

9. Serve the Spinach and Quinoa Stuffed Bell Peppers hot, garnished with chopped fresh cilantro, avocado slices, sour cream, or salsa if desired.

These Spinach and Quinoa Stuffed Bell Peppers are a nutritious and satisfying vegetarian meal. They're packed with protein, fiber, and flavor, making them a delicious option for lunch or dinner. Plus, they're a great way to use up leftover quinoa and veggies!

**Baked Salmon with Asparagus**

Ingredients:

- 4 salmon fillets, skin-on or skinless, about 6 oz each
- 1 bunch asparagus, woody ends trimmed
- 2 tablespoons olive oil
- 2 cloves garlic, minced
- 1 teaspoon lemon zest
- 1 tablespoon lemon juice
- Salt and pepper to taste
- Optional garnish: chopped fresh parsley, lemon slices

Instructions:

Preheat Oven:

1. Preheat your oven to 400°F (200°C). Line a baking sheet with parchment paper or aluminum foil for easy cleanup.

Prepare Salmon:

2. Pat the salmon fillets dry with paper towels and place them on the prepared baking sheet. If using skin-on salmon, arrange them skin-side down. Season the salmon fillets with salt and pepper to taste.

Prepare Asparagus:

3. Place trimmed asparagus spears on the baking sheet around the salmon fillets.

Make Lemon Garlic Mixture:

4. In a small bowl, whisk together olive oil, minced garlic, lemon zest, and lemon juice. Drizzle the mixture over the salmon fillets and asparagus.

Bake:

5. Place the baking sheet in the preheated oven and bake for 12-15 minutes, or until the salmon is cooked through and flakes easily with a fork, and the asparagus is tender but still crisp.

Serve:

6. Remove the baked salmon and asparagus from the oven. Optionally, garnish with chopped fresh parsley and lemon slices.

Enjoy!

7. Serve the Baked Salmon with Asparagus hot as a delicious and nutritious meal.

This Baked Salmon with Asparagus recipe is quick and easy to make, yet elegant enough for a special occasion. It's a healthy and flavorful dish that's perfect for busy weeknights or entertaining guests. Enjoy the tender and flaky salmon paired with the vibrant and crisp asparagus, all infused with the bright flavors of lemon and garlic.

**Vegetable and Lentil Shepherd's Pie**

Ingredients:

For the Lentil Filling:

- 1 cup dried green or brown lentils, rinsed
- 3 cups vegetable broth
- 1 tablespoon olive oil
- 1 onion, diced
- 2 carrots, diced
- 2 celery stalks, diced
- 2 cloves garlic, minced
- 1 teaspoon dried thyme
- 1 teaspoon dried rosemary
- 1 teaspoon paprika
- Salt and pepper to taste
- 1 cup frozen peas
- 1 cup frozen corn
- 2 tablespoons tomato paste
- 2 tablespoons soy sauce or tamari (optional, for umami flavor)

For the Mashed Potato Topping:

- 4 large potatoes, peeled and chopped into chunks
- 1/4 cup unsweetened non-dairy milk (such as almond milk or oat milk)
- 2 tablespoons vegan butter or olive oil
- Salt and pepper to taste

Instructions:

Cook Lentils:

1. In a medium saucepan, combine rinsed lentils and vegetable broth. Bring to a boil, then reduce heat to low, cover, and simmer for 20-25 minutes, or until the lentils are tender and most of the liquid is absorbed.

Prepare Mashed Potatoes:

2. While the lentils are cooking, place chopped potatoes in a large pot and cover with water. Bring to a boil, then reduce heat to medium and simmer for 15-20 minutes, or until the potatoes are fork-tender. Drain the cooked potatoes and return them to the pot. Add non-dairy milk, vegan butter or olive oil, salt, and pepper. Mash the potatoes until smooth and creamy. Set aside.

Preheat Oven:

3. Preheat your oven to 375°F (190°C).

Prepare Lentil Filling:

4. In a large skillet, heat olive oil over medium heat. Add diced onion, carrots, and celery. Cook until softened, about 5-7 minutes. Add minced garlic, dried thyme, dried rosemary, paprika, salt, and pepper. Cook for another 1-2 minutes until fragrant. Add frozen peas, frozen corn, cooked lentils (along with any remaining broth), tomato paste, and soy sauce (if using). Stir to combine and cook for an additional 5 minutes, allowing the flavors to meld together. Adjust seasoning to taste.

Assemble Shepherd's Pie:

5. Transfer the lentil and vegetable mixture to a large baking dish. Spread the mashed potatoes evenly over the top of the lentil mixture, creating a smooth layer.

Bake:

6. Place the baking dish in the preheated oven and bake for 25-30 minutes, or until the mashed potato topping is lightly golden and the filling is bubbly.

Serve:

7. Remove the Shepherd's Pie from the oven and let it cool slightly before serving.

Enjoy!

8. Serve the Vegetable and Lentil Shepherd's Pie hot as a comforting and satisfying meal.

This Vegetable and Lentil Shepherd's Pie is a wholesome and nutritious dish that's perfect for a cozy dinner. It's packed with protein, fiber, and flavor, making it a satisfying option for vegetarians and meat-eaters alike. Enjoy the hearty lentil and vegetable filling topped with creamy mashed potatoes for a delicious and comforting meal.

**Chicken and Mushroom Stroganoff**

Ingredients:

- 1 lb boneless, skinless chicken breasts, cut into bite-sized pieces
- 8 oz mushrooms, sliced (such as cremini or button mushrooms)
- 1 onion, finely chopped
- 2 cloves garlic, minced
- 2 tablespoons olive oil
- 2 tablespoons all-purpose flour
- 1 cup chicken broth
- 1 cup sour cream
- 2 teaspoons Dijon mustard
- 1 teaspoon paprika
- Salt and pepper to taste
- Fresh parsley, chopped, for garnish
- Cooked egg noodles or rice, for serving

Instructions:

1. Cook Chicken:
   In a large skillet, heat 1 tablespoon of olive oil over medium-high heat. Add the chicken pieces and cook until golden brown and cooked through, about 5-7 minutes. Remove the chicken from the skillet and set aside.
2. Cook Mushrooms and Onions:
   In the same skillet, add the remaining tablespoon of olive oil. Add the sliced mushrooms and chopped onion. Cook until the mushrooms are golden brown and the onions are softened, about 5-7 minutes. Add the minced garlic and cook for an additional 1-2 minutes.
3. Make Sauce:
   Sprinkle the flour over the mushrooms and onions. Stir well to combine and cook for 1-2 minutes. Slowly pour in the chicken broth, stirring constantly to prevent lumps from forming. Bring the mixture to a simmer and cook until slightly thickened, about 2-3 minutes.
4. Combine Chicken and Sauce:
   Return the cooked chicken to the skillet. Stir in the sour cream, Dijon mustard, and paprika. Season with salt and pepper to taste. Cook for another 2-3 minutes, or until heated through and the sauce is creamy.

5. Serve:
   Serve the Chicken and Mushroom Stroganoff hot over cooked egg noodles or rice. Garnish with chopped fresh parsley.
6. Enjoy!
   Enjoy this creamy and flavorful Chicken and Mushroom Stroganoff as a comforting and satisfying meal.

This Chicken and Mushroom Stroganoff is perfect for a cozy dinner at home. The creamy sauce, tender chicken, and earthy mushrooms come together beautifully for a delicious and comforting dish that the whole family will love.

**Eggplant and Chickpea Stew**

Ingredients:

- 1 large eggplant, diced into cubes
- 1 can (15 oz) chickpeas, drained and rinsed
- 1 onion, diced
- 2 cloves garlic, minced
- 1 can (14.5 oz) diced tomatoes
- 2 cups vegetable broth
- 1 teaspoon ground cumin
- 1 teaspoon ground coriander
- 1 teaspoon smoked paprika
- 1/2 teaspoon dried thyme
- Salt and pepper to taste
- 2 tablespoons olive oil
- Fresh parsley or cilantro, chopped (for garnish)
- Cooked couscous or rice, for serving

Instructions:

1. Prepare Eggplant:
   Place the diced eggplant in a colander and sprinkle with salt. Let it sit for about 15-20 minutes to release excess moisture. Rinse the eggplant under cold water and pat dry with paper towels.
2. Saute Onion and Garlic:
   Heat olive oil in a large pot or Dutch oven over medium heat. Add diced onion and minced garlic. Cook until softened and fragrant, about 3-4 minutes.
3. Add Spices:
   Stir in ground cumin, ground coriander, smoked paprika, dried thyme, salt, and pepper. Cook for another minute to toast the spices and release their flavors.
4. Cook Eggplant and Chickpeas:
   Add the diced eggplant and drained chickpeas to the pot. Stir to combine with the onion and spices. Cook for 5-7 minutes, until the eggplant starts to soften.
5. Add Tomatoes and Broth:
   Pour in the diced tomatoes (with their juices) and vegetable broth. Stir well to combine. Bring the mixture to a simmer.

6. Simmer:
   Reduce heat to low, cover, and let the stew simmer for 20-25 minutes, stirring occasionally, until the eggplant is tender and the flavors have melded together.
7. Adjust Seasoning:
   Taste the stew and adjust the seasoning with more salt and pepper if needed.
8. Serve:
   Serve the Eggplant and Chickpea Stew hot, garnished with chopped fresh parsley or cilantro. Serve over cooked couscous or rice.
9. Enjoy!
   Enjoy this hearty and flavorful Eggplant and Chickpea Stew as a satisfying vegetarian meal.

This Eggplant and Chickpea Stew is packed with protein, fiber, and flavor. It's a comforting and nutritious dish that's perfect for a cozy dinner on a chilly evening. The combination of tender eggplant, hearty chickpeas, and aromatic spices creates a delicious and satisfying stew that everyone will love.

**Tuna and White Bean Salad**

Ingredients:

- 2 cans (5 oz each) tuna, drained
- 2 cans (15 oz each) white beans (such as cannellini beans), drained and rinsed
- 1/2 red onion, finely chopped
- 1 celery stalk, finely chopped
- 1/4 cup chopped fresh parsley
- 2 tablespoons lemon juice
- 2 tablespoons extra virgin olive oil
- 1 teaspoon Dijon mustard
- Salt and pepper to taste
- Optional: cherry tomatoes, sliced cucumber, olives, mixed greens for serving

Instructions:

Prepare Tuna and Beans:

1. In a large mixing bowl, combine drained tuna and white beans.

Add Vegetables:

2. Add finely chopped red onion, celery, and chopped fresh parsley to the bowl with the tuna and beans.

Make Dressing:

3. In a small bowl, whisk together lemon juice, extra virgin olive oil, Dijon mustard, salt, and pepper to make the dressing.

Combine:

4. Pour the dressing over the tuna, white beans, and vegetables in the mixing bowl. Gently toss until everything is well combined and evenly coated with the dressing.

Chill:

5. Cover the bowl with plastic wrap or transfer the salad to an airtight container. Chill in the refrigerator for at least 30 minutes to allow the flavors to meld together.

Serve:

6. Serve the Tuna and White Bean Salad chilled, either on its own or over a bed of mixed greens. Optionally, garnish with cherry tomatoes, sliced cucumber, olives, or your favorite salad toppings.

Enjoy!

7. Enjoy this delicious and nutritious Tuna and White Bean Salad as a satisfying and protein-packed meal.

This Tuna and White Bean Salad is quick and easy to make, yet packed with flavor and nutrients. It's perfect for a light lunch, a quick dinner, or meal prep for busy weekdays. Plus, it's versatile, so feel free to customize it with your favorite vegetables and toppings.

**Lemon Garlic Chicken and Green Beans**

Ingredients:

For the Chicken:

- 4 boneless, skinless chicken breasts
- 2 tablespoons olive oil
- 4 cloves garlic, minced
- Zest of 1 lemon
- Juice of 1 lemon
- Salt and pepper to taste
- Fresh parsley, chopped (for garnish)

For the Green Beans:

- 1 lb fresh green beans, trimmed
- 2 tablespoons butter or olive oil
- 2 cloves garlic, minced
- Juice of 1/2 lemon
- Salt and pepper to taste

Instructions:

Preheat Oven:

1. Preheat your oven to 400°F (200°C).

Prepare Chicken:

2. Place the chicken breasts on a cutting board and pat them dry with paper towels. Season both sides of the chicken breasts with salt and pepper.

Cook Chicken:

3. In a large oven-safe skillet, heat olive oil over medium-high heat. Add minced garlic and cook for about 1 minute until fragrant. Add the chicken breasts to the skillet and sear on each side for 2-3 minutes until golden brown.

Add Lemon Zest and Juice:

4. Sprinkle lemon zest over the chicken breasts, then squeeze the lemon juice over them. Transfer the skillet to the preheated oven and bake for 15-20 minutes, or until the chicken is cooked through and reaches an internal temperature of 165°F (75°C).

Prepare Green Beans:

5. While the chicken is baking, prepare the green beans. In a separate skillet, melt butter (or heat olive oil) over medium heat. Add minced garlic and cook for about 1 minute until fragrant. Add trimmed green beans to the skillet and sauté for 5-7 minutes, or until they are crisp-tender.

Add Lemon Juice:

6. Squeeze lemon juice over the green beans and season with salt and pepper to taste. Toss well to combine.

Serve:

7. Once the chicken is cooked through, remove the skillet from the oven. Serve the Lemon Garlic Chicken and Green Beans hot, garnished with chopped fresh parsley.

Enjoy!

8. Enjoy this flavorful and nutritious Lemon Garlic Chicken and Green Beans as a satisfying meal.

This Lemon Garlic Chicken and Green Beans recipe is quick and easy to make, yet full of bright flavors. The tender and juicy chicken pairs perfectly with the crisp-tender green beans, all infused with the zesty and aromatic lemon garlic sauce. It's a delicious and wholesome meal that's perfect for any day of the week!

**Veggie-Packed Quinoa Pilaf**

Ingredients:

- 1 cup quinoa, rinsed
- 2 cups vegetable broth or water
- 2 tablespoons olive oil
- 1 onion, finely chopped
- 2 cloves garlic, minced
- 1 carrot, diced
- 1 red bell pepper, diced
- 1 zucchini, diced
- 1 cup frozen peas
- 1 teaspoon ground cumin
- 1 teaspoon ground coriander
- 1/2 teaspoon turmeric
- Salt and pepper to taste
- Fresh parsley or cilantro, chopped (for garnish)

Instructions:

Cook Quinoa:

1. In a medium saucepan, combine rinsed quinoa and vegetable broth (or water). Bring to a boil, then reduce heat to low, cover, and simmer for 15-20 minutes, or until the quinoa is cooked and the liquid is absorbed. Fluff with a fork and set aside.

Prepare Vegetables:

2. While the quinoa is cooking, heat olive oil in a large skillet over medium heat. Add finely chopped onion and minced garlic. Cook until softened and fragrant, about 3-4 minutes.

Add Carrot and Bell Pepper:

3. Add diced carrot and diced red bell pepper to the skillet. Cook for 5-6 minutes, or until the vegetables start to soften.

Add Zucchini and Peas:

4. Stir in diced zucchini and frozen peas. Cook for an additional 3-4 minutes, or until all the vegetables are tender.

Season:

5. Sprinkle ground cumin, ground coriander, turmeric, salt, and pepper over the vegetables. Stir well to combine and coat the vegetables with the spices.

Combine with Quinoa:

6. Add the cooked quinoa to the skillet with the vegetables. Stir well to combine all the ingredients.

Adjust Seasoning:

7. Taste the quinoa pilaf and adjust the seasoning with more salt and pepper if needed.

Serve:

8. Transfer the Veggie-Packed Quinoa Pilaf to a serving dish. Garnish with chopped fresh parsley or cilantro.

Enjoy!

9. Serve the quinoa pilaf hot as a delicious and nutritious side dish or main course.

This Veggie-Packed Quinoa Pilaf is loaded with nutritious vegetables and fragrant spices, making it a flavorful and satisfying dish. Enjoy it as a standalone meal or serve it alongside your favorite protein for a complete and balanced meal. It's perfect for meal prep and makes great leftovers for lunch the next day!

**Balsamic Glazed Roasted Vegetables**

Ingredients:

- 2 cups Brussels sprouts, trimmed and halved
- 2 cups carrots, peeled and sliced into rounds
- 2 cups sweet potatoes, peeled and diced
- 1 red onion, sliced
- 2 tablespoons olive oil
- Salt and pepper to taste
- 3 tablespoons balsamic vinegar
- 2 tablespoons honey or maple syrup (for vegan option)
- 2 cloves garlic, minced
- 1 teaspoon dried thyme (optional)
- Fresh parsley, chopped (for garnish)

Instructions:

1. Preheat Oven:
   Preheat your oven to 400°F (200°C).
2. Prepare Vegetables:
   In a large mixing bowl, combine Brussels sprouts, carrots, sweet potatoes, and red onion. Drizzle with olive oil and season with salt and pepper to taste. Toss well to coat all the vegetables evenly with the oil and seasoning.
3. Roast Vegetables:
   Spread the vegetables in a single layer on a large baking sheet. Roast in the preheated oven for 25-30 minutes, or until the vegetables are tender and starting to caramelize around the edges. Stir halfway through cooking to ensure even roasting.
4. Make Balsamic Glaze:
   While the vegetables are roasting, prepare the balsamic glaze. In a small saucepan, combine balsamic vinegar, honey or maple syrup, minced garlic, and dried thyme (if using). Bring the mixture to a simmer over medium heat. Cook for 3-4 minutes, stirring occasionally, until the glaze has thickened slightly. Remove from heat.
5. Glaze Vegetables:
   Once the vegetables are roasted, drizzle the balsamic glaze over them. Toss gently to coat the vegetables evenly with the glaze.

6. Serve:
   Transfer the Balsamic Glazed Roasted Vegetables to a serving dish. Garnish with chopped fresh parsley for a pop of color and freshness.
7. Enjoy!
   Serve the vegetables hot as a flavorful and nutritious side dish or vegetarian main course.

These Balsamic Glazed Roasted Vegetables are packed with flavor and make a beautiful addition to any meal. The combination of sweet potatoes, Brussels sprouts, carrots, and red onion, roasted to perfection and coated in a tangy-sweet balsamic glaze, is sure to impress your taste buds. Enjoy the deliciousness!

**Spiced Lentil and Carrot Soup**

Ingredients:

- 1 cup dried red lentils, rinsed and drained
- 2 tablespoons olive oil
- 1 onion, chopped
- 2 cloves garlic, minced
- 2 large carrots, peeled and diced
- 1 teaspoon ground cumin
- 1/2 teaspoon ground turmeric
- 1/2 teaspoon ground coriander
- 1/4 teaspoon ground cinnamon
- 1/4 teaspoon cayenne pepper (optional, for heat)
- 4 cups vegetable broth
- 1 (14.5 oz) can diced tomatoes
- Salt and pepper to taste
- Fresh cilantro or parsley, chopped (for garnish)
- Greek yogurt or coconut milk (for serving, optional)

Instructions:

1. Saute Aromatics:
   Heat olive oil in a large pot over medium heat. Add chopped onion and cook until softened, about 3-4 minutes. Add minced garlic and cook for another 1-2 minutes until fragrant.
2. Add Vegetables and Spices:
   Stir in diced carrots, ground cumin, ground turmeric, ground coriander, ground cinnamon, and cayenne pepper (if using). Cook for 2-3 minutes, stirring occasionally, to toast the spices and coat the vegetables.
3. Add Lentils and Liquid:
   Add rinsed red lentils, vegetable broth, and diced tomatoes (with their juices) to the pot. Stir well to combine.
4. Simmer:
   Bring the soup to a boil, then reduce the heat to low. Cover and simmer for 20-25 minutes, or until the lentils and carrots are tender.
5. Blend (Optional):
   For a smoother consistency, use an immersion blender to blend the soup directly

in the pot until smooth. Alternatively, transfer the soup in batches to a blender and blend until smooth, then return it to the pot.
6. Season:
   Season the soup with salt and pepper to taste. Adjust the seasoning as needed.
7. Serve:
   Ladle the Spiced Lentil and Carrot Soup into bowls. Garnish with chopped fresh cilantro or parsley.
8. Enjoy!
   Serve the soup hot, optionally topped with a dollop of Greek yogurt or a drizzle of coconut milk for added creaminess.

This Spiced Lentil and Carrot Soup is hearty, nutritious, and bursting with flavor from the aromatic spices. It's perfect for a cozy meal on a chilly day and makes great leftovers for lunch the next day. Enjoy the comforting warmth and deliciousness of this soup!

www.ingramcontent.com/pod-product-compliance
Lightning Source LLC
LaVergne TN
LVHW061938070526
838199LV00060B/3866